C O M P L E T E
Woodfinishing

COMPLETE
Woodfinishing

IAN HOSKER

GUILD OF MASTER CRAFTSMAN PUBLICATIONS

First published 1993 by
Guild of Master Craftsman Publications Ltd,
166 High Street, Lewes, East Sussex BN7 1XU

© Ian Hosker 1993

ISBN 0 946819 33 5

Illustrations © Tim Benké 1993

Photography by Ian Hosker, except where credited
otherwise.
Photographs of woodgrain throughout courtesy of
Ecological Trading Company Ltd.
Cover photograph by David Maxwell.

Designed by Ian Hunt Design

Printed and bound in Hong Kong under
the supervision of
Mandarin Offset, London.

DEDICATION
To Barbara, Samantha and David

Contents

Acknowledgements

It is customary to pay some tribute to all those who made it an easier task to write this book than would otherwise have been the case. The following individuals and organizations are listed because their help was invaluable.

For valuable technical information: MacPhersons Paints; DeVilbiss Ransburg; Cuprinol; Binks-Bullows; Clarke Group; Sonneborn & Rieck Ltd; Fiddes & Son.

For photographs for this book: Black & Decker; Interwood; Binks-Bullows; DeVilbiss Ransburg; Arco Ltd; Rentokil; Racal; Cuprinol; Keith Welters; Geoff Ford; Keith Rowley; Liberon Waxes; Hamilton Acorn Ltd; Startrite Tools; GT French Polishing; Ecological Trading Company; George Justice; Hitachi (UK) Ltd; A. S. Handover Ltd; Machine Mart.

Eleven years of teaching the subjects of furniture restoration and woodfinishing provides a plethora of people who contribute in an anonymous way. The book grew out of the many requests for information that was detailed enough to be worth the effort of reading, but which was not so technical as to be unintelligible. Some areas of this book developed from course notes and handbooks. So, to those numerous advisers, critics and eternal sources of ideas and wisdom who are my past and present students, thanks!

Barbara Hosker has been very forbearing throughout the process of writing, and has provided very practical help and support throughout the process. Her hands are also much nicer than mine, and you will find that they appear in a number of illustrations!

Introduction

The art of the woodcraftsman has acquired a respect and prestige in recent years that would almost certainly bring a wry smile to the face of any craftsman who served his time and practised his craft in the 1920s and 1930s. He knows only too well how the prestige and demand for his skills declined during those years. Why was this so? Simply, the demands of a mass market and the effect this had on production techniques made it inevitable.

Today, though, there is once again a hierarchy of skill and prestige – when a craftsman is called a cabinetmaker rather than a joiner or carpenter. I have been teaching furniture restoration and French polishing for some considerable time, and every year without fail the same deference to these skills is exhibited by beginners in a way that makes me wonder why it is so.

I suppose the answer has to lie in the relationship (real and assumed) between the craftsman and the raw materials, made even more significant by the very nature of the wood itself, i.e. it was once a living organism. It is a decorative craft as well as a functional one (who gets really excited and marvels at the beauty of their central heating plumbing?). The 'artistry' associated with woodcraftsmanship can only be achieved if the craftsman has a genuine and deep understanding of the qualities of his materials, and a 'feel' for them – skills can be taught, but the relationship between practitioner and materials is something else again.

This book has no pretentions in the direction of turning you into a craftsman – that inner commitment and understanding is beyond the capabilities of any teacher to transmit – but it should give you a good grounding in the materials and processes of woodfinishing.

The art of the finisher is particularly important, as a good finisher is able to turn a not-too-inspiring piece of work into something very different indeed – even to the point of disguising the minor errors of the woodcraftsman. Yet it is also an area that seems to create an inordinate number of difficulties for people: many a good piece of cabinet work has been ruined by poor polishing.

I hope that this book goes some way towards dispelling the mystique that seems to surround woodfinishing and helps you develop your skills.

The Right Finish for the Job

Having finally got around to converting into a reality that idea for a table that has been knocking around your head for the last few months, how are you going to finish it? Surely you weren't planning to slap a couple of coats of polyurethane on it and hope that it will look OK! You were? Let's look at this a little more closely.

There is absolutely nothing wrong with polyurethane, as you will discover later in the book, but perhaps something else is better. But before finding out what, if anything, is better, why do we bother with a finish in the first place? Essentially, we put on some form of colouring and/or coating material:

▌ To enhance the natural beauty of wood's grain texture and surface markings (referred to as figure).

▌ To produce an even colour and surface that is pleasing to look at and which fits in well with its surroundings.

▌ To protect the wood from a wide variety of things that will destroy, damage or disfigure it in some way.

It is a well-worn cliché, used in all books on woodfinishing, that many a good piece of woodcraftsmanship is ruined by poor staining and polishing. For generations the craft of the cabinetmaker and that of the polisher have been separate, and perhaps that should tell us something. However, there is no real excuse for bodging. Not everyone can French polish, but there are alternatives that can make the work look just as good. So, why is there this problem?

▌ Lack of knowledge, skill and experience of the wide range of finishing materials that are now available to both professional and amateur.

▌ Lack of planning; finishing is often left out of the 'thinking it through' process; consequently, very little attention is given to it.

Planning is a matter of good working practice. Before you touch the first piece of wood to start your project, you should already know what its final surface will look like because you will have asked yourself a number of questions which will set the criteria for choosing a finish. The sort of questions you should ask are:

▌ Will it have to be a particular colour?

▌ Will it be handled a great deal?

▌ Will it be subjected to possible water or alcohol spillages?

▌ Will it be subjected to having hot objects placed on it?

▌ Will it look better as a high gloss, low lustre or totally matt?

▌ Is the object under consideration going to be indoors or out?

▌ What skills do I possess?

▌ Is the nature of the wood itself going to determine the best method of finishing (i.e. is there an attractive figure that needs to be brought out, or is the wood likely to reject certain finishes)?

▌ Is there a traditional way of finishing this particular wood?

▌ Does the piece have to match other items?

Not all the questions need be asked every time, and there may even be others that occur to you at the time, but the need to include some thought on finishing at the planning stage of your project cannot be overstressed, as it may sometimes influence other factors. For example, it is sometimes better to stain and polish components before assembly, and without forward planning you could make life difficult for yourself.

**Fig 1.1 Varnish on this exterior door has broken down,
leading to rainwater penetration.**

THE WRONG FINISH

It is not just a question of making life a little bit easier; there can be unfortunate and disappointing consequences if the wrong type of finish is applied or if the type of stain is incompatible with the polish material or solvent, or if incorrect surface preparation has taken place.

Fig 1.1 shows an exterior door where the varnish is peeling off and there is bad staining due to moisture. Normal internal polyurethane varnish is unsuitable, as the constant movement of the door, expanding and contracting as atmospheric conditions change, causes it to crack through not being very flexible. This allows water to penetrate and lift the varnish. (As a process, it can be a very effective stripper!) Alternatively, it could be that moisture was trapped in the wood prior to finishing, or the stain used was not quite dry. The result would be the same. One of the new breed of micro-porous varnishes would have been better (*see* Chapter 8).

Fig 1.2 shows the badly ring-marked and scratched surface of a French polished table. This very beautiful but vulnerable finish is not resistant to heat, alcohol or moisture. Perhaps, in this case, an acid-cured lacquer (*see* Chapter 9), or even a burnished polyurethane varnish (*see* Chapter 8) might have been better.

At the end of this chapter there is a flowchart to help you decide upon the best finish for the job in hand. By answering the questions, you will be led step by step to those that seem to fit the bill. It will also direct you to the appropriate sections of the book where you can read up on your chosen finish.

Chapters 4 and 5 are obligatory reading, as the procedures are the same, no matter what you plan to do, and there is some information regarding certain stains being potentially incompatible with the final polish, which should be checked before continuing.

TRADITIONAL FINISHING OF
SOME TIMBERS

Just because something is traditionally done does not, of course, bind you to doing the same, but it might bring some influence to bear on your eventual choice, as traditions are based on what experience shows to work. Oak, pine and teak seem to please the eye more when they are finished to a low lustre. Oak has a rustic image, and its coarse grain texture and medullary ray figuring (on quarter-sawn boards) are certainly shown off at their best if the grain is left open (i.e. no grain filler has been used) and there is no high build-up of polish. This creates the impression that you are touching the wood itself when you run your fingers over it (as most people would be tempted to do).

Pine is a curious one, in that some people will spend staggering amounts of money for a stripped pine piece. In fact, pine furniture was quite ordinary and cheap, often relegated to the servants' working and living areas. In such situations it was usually quite bare, and kitchen tables, in particular, were scrubbed after use, eventually taking on a mellow, burnished look that no polish could possibly reproduce. Pine was also used as a base for high quality painted furniture; a number of coats of gesso were applied, and were then sanded to mirror smoothness.

Walnut, mahogany and rosewood look superb under carefully applied French polish, where the optical qualities seem to enhance the attractive and dramatic figures characteristic of these timbers.

Oak was traditionally waxed, oiled or simply burnished, its rustic surface texture and figure being allowed to speak for themselves.

In the end, however, it is your decision as to how you finish your project, so long as at the end of the day it is pleasing to look at and is durable enough for its purpose.

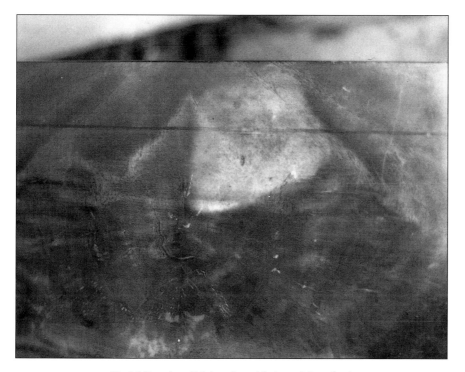

Fig 1.2 French polish is vulnerable to moisture, heat, alcohol and other solvents.

CHOOSING A FINISH

Table 1 can be used to guide you towards an appropriate finish for the job in hand. However, there may be other overriding factors to take into account.

Starting at the top, follow the arrows that give the appropriate criteria. For example, if the surface needs to be durable, you are led to the questions 'internal?' or 'external?' Assuming the work is external, is it liable to be absorbing a lot of moisture, or do you suspect that moisture may be there already? If the answer is yes, do you want a hard finish or a finish that is non-coating? Hard finish leads you to use microporous materials, and non-coating leads to solvent- or oil-based preservative.

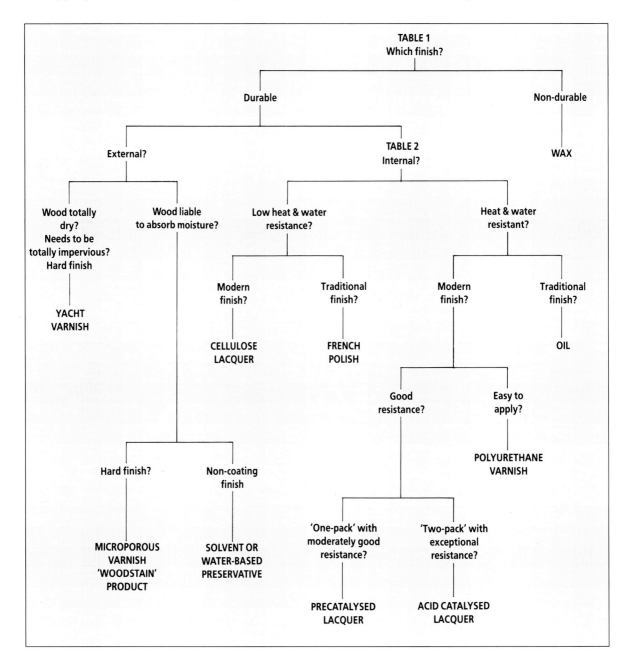

As I say, this is only a guide, and you may find that when you turn to the appropriate chapters the finish may not be exactly what you are looking for; an alternative should then be sought, but you may need to compromise on specifications. For example, you may decide on French polish, and therefore compromise on heat and water resistance.

MATERIALS AND METHODS

The great thing about finishing as a craft is that the tools and materials required to perform the task are relatively few, compared to other crafts associated with woodworking. Nevertheless, a thorough understanding of what they are and how they are used is vital if you are to produce a decent finish. Where appropriate, an explanation of methods and materials has been provided.

Finally, at the end of the book, Chapter 16 is devoted to recipes for making polishes, cleaners and revivers, and a number of other useful substances that the woodfinisher may need and which can be successfully home-made in small or large batches.

METHOD OF WORKING

It has already been mentioned that many problems and disappointments arise through poor planning, or even no real planning at all. You must know in advance what procedures are needed. You need to be meticulous in your approach to the work and, above all, do not rush things. If a varnish requires six hours to dry sufficiently to allow another coat, then leave it for six hours. This may seem patronising, but, believe me, the temptation can sometimes be irresistibly overwhelming: on many occasions I have been so pushed for time that I have had to walk away from the job and put it out of my mind to reduce the frustration.

In general, the order of working is as follows:

■ Prepare the surface by filling or repairing blemishes, and smoothing.

■ Stain (if required).

■ Fill the grain (if required).

■ Apply an initial coat of polish.

■ Correct any colour errors (if appropriate).

■ Apply finishing coats of polish.

It is usual (except in the case of waxing and oiling) to gently rub down the surface between coats, partly to remove adhering particles but also to provide a key for the subsequent coat.

COMPATIBILITY

An object lesson: I was quietly working away in my workshop one morning when I received an unexpected caller – another woodcraftsman. He had a problem. Some months before, this man had polished bar tops in a local pub, and was now in the process of taking the licensee to the small claims court for nonpayment. How could this concern me? The customer was, it seems, refusing to pay because of faulty workmanship on a grand scale: he claimed that on one of the bar tops the lacquer had totally disappeared.

I agreed to this man's request to act as an independent assessor and simply walk into the pub, buy a drink and stand at the bar and view it. Sadly, the licensee was correct. The wood was indeed almost totally devoid of lacquer, and where it was present, the surface was flaky and unstable.

On further investigation, it seems that this could well have been a case of incompatibility. Not only do you need to consider the procedural element of the equation, but you must also pay a great deal of attention to ensuring that the different materials you may use are compatible.

CHAPTER 2

Power Sanding

trictly speaking, it could be argued that this chapter does not belong to this book, as the subject may well be considered as woodwork and not woodfinishing. However, a great deal will be made of meticulous preparation of substrates (the material to be finished) prior to finishing, and this chapter is justified, as all woodworkers, whether amateur or professional, are well aware of the benefits offered by power tools in taking out the hard work and tedium associated with hand work.

My own view is that, in the end, it is necessary to resort to hand finishing if the 'ultimate' surface is wanted. Of course, this is too labour-intensive for commercial production techniques, although there is still room at the top end of the market for skilled visual inspection and manual correction of blemishes.

Excluding the process of applying the polish itself, power is used at two stages in the finishing process:

▮ to produce a very smooth surface on the bare substrate prior to staining and polishing

▮ to cut back intermediate coats of polish.

There are three main types of sanding machines: disc, belt and orbital. Because the process of sanding is based on scratching away the surface with an abrasive material, it is fairly obvious that the abrasive will leave its own marks. It is important that the abrasion takes place along the grain, otherwise there will be marks that show through the final finish, no matter how careful you have been. (*See* Chapter 4 for more details.)

Disc Sander

This tool has no place in fine woodfinishing. It is a rough tool designed for indiscriminate removal of material without any regard for the quality of the final surface. Fig 2.1 shows the murderous effect of a disc sander on a flat substrate.

As the disc rotates it cuts deeply across the grain, no matter how the abrasive is presented to the substrate. Such damage, for that is what it is, is virtually impossible to repair satisfactorily. Using a fine grade of abrasive will not help either, as any cutting across the grain will always show through the final finish, especially if it is gloss.

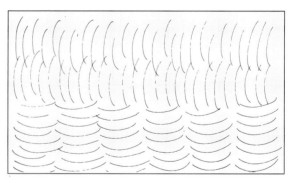

Fig 2.1 (b) Effect of disc sanders on the surface of wood (top view).

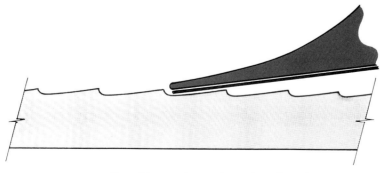

Fig 2.1 (a) Effect of disc sanders on the surface of wood (side view).

These sanders must never be used on veneered work, as their action is so rapid and severe you will cut through to the groundwork before there is any time to think about it.

Belt Sander

As its name implies, a belt of abrasive runs over two rollers, with the working face running over a smooth metal base plate which presses the belt on to the substrate. Industrial sanding machines can be quite huge (*see* Fig 2.2).

Hand-held sanders (*see* Fig 2.3) are very useful for the initial preparation prior to hand sanding or using an orbital sander. They are designed to give rapid removal of material, and are frequently used to prepare the surface after it has been planed. As will be seen in Chapter 4, machine planing does not produce a satisfactory surface, and belt sanding is often a really good way of quickly smoothing out the blemishes. A good craftsman with a well-honed and finely adjusted smoothing plane can produce an almost perfect surface by hand. Belt sanders are not suitable for use on a veneered surface because of the rapid removal of wood.

PHOTOGRAPH COURTESY OF INTERWOOD LTD.

Fig 2.2 (a) Table belt sander.

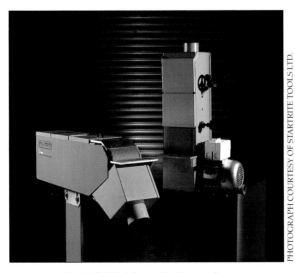

PHOTOGRAPH COURTESY OF STARTRITE TOOLS LTD.

Fig 2.2 (b) Linisher with disc sander.

Fig 2.3 (a) Hand-held belt sander with a sanding frame to control depth of cut on flat surfaces.

Fig 2.3 (b) Hand-held belt sander without a sanding frame.

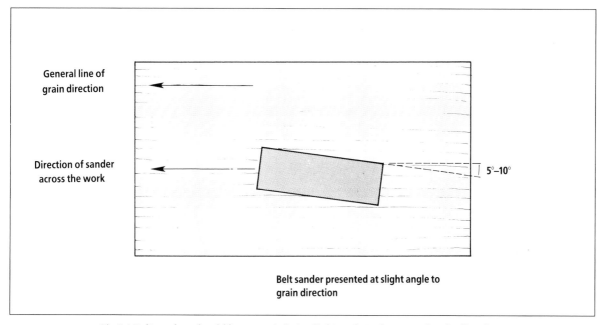

General line of grain direction

Direction of sander across the work

5°–10°

Belt sander presented at slight angle to grain direction

Fig 2.4 Belt sanders should be presented at a slight angle to the general grain direction.

As you push the machine along the wood (using only the weight of the machine itself, with virtually no downward pressure), the area of the belt in contact with the substrate opposes the movement of the tool. This gives two advantages: friction, and thereby the cutting action, is increased, and you have better control.

Though it might seem a contradiction of what was said earlier about not using abrasive material across the grain, the belt sander does work better if it is allowed to cut at a slight angle to the grain direction (*see* Fig 2.4).

Final sanding is now achieved either by hand or through the use of an orbital sander.

PHOTOGRAPH COURTESY OF BLACK & DECKER LTD.

Fig 2.5 An orbital sander.

Orbital Sander

This is a final smoothing tool, rather than a machine designed to remove a large amount of material (*see* Fig 2.5). Consequently, it should always be used with fine grades of abrasive paper.

The machine operates by rotating its base around a fixed position (hence the term orbital), so that each grain of abrasive actually rotates in a circle over the substrate, effectively scouring the surface. This is done at very high speed, and the diameter of rotation is very small indeed (*see*

Fig 2.6). Problems arise if you use an orbital sander with coarse paper grades, as the grains of abrasive leave behind a very large number of tiny circular scratches that are very difficult to remedy later.

Another point to bear in mind is that it is inadvisable to use excessive pressure, as this will only lead to a poor quality surface being produced; undue and detrimental loading of the motor will occur as well, reducing the life of the tool. As with the belt sander, use only the pressure caused by the weight of the machine.

Provided you only use fine grades of abrasive paper, the action of an orbital sander is very gentle and can be used with reasonable confidence on veneered work (but still take care when refinishing pieces, as the veneer is probably very thin).

During use, orbital sanders can be moved over the whole surface in any direction. The rotation of the base makes the rule of moving only along the grain pretty pointless.

Palm sanders are orbital sanders small enough to fit snugly into the palm of one hand, which makes them useful for small and awkward areas, such as the insides of drawers (*see* Fig 2.7).

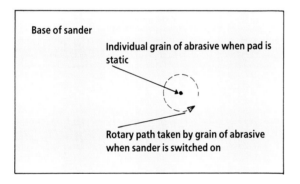

Base of sander

Individual grain of abrasive when pad is static

Rotary path taken by grain of abrasive when sander is switched on

Fig 2.6 Orbital sanders operate by vibrating the abrasive pad in a small circular path at very high speed.

PHOTOGRAPH COURTESY OF BLACK & DECKER LTD.

Fig 2.7 A palm sander.

Power sanding machines should be kept on the move all the time and not be allowed to dwell on any single spot for any length of time, or you will create hollows or cut through veneers. You should stop the machine as dust begins to build up on the surface, and clear it away. The dust not only contains wood fibres, but also a few grains of abrasive mixed up. If this mixture is allowed to accumulate beneath the sanding pad, it may scratch the surface and undo the work you have put in attempting to create the 'perfect' smoothness.

USEFUL FEATURES OF
POWER SANDERS

As a general rule, you should always buy the best tools and equipment that you can afford; if you intend to do a lot of work, it does pay to invest in quality. 'Horses for courses' applies here, as the quality of powered equipment varies markedly; the market consists of different levels of need and depth of pockets. Not long ago, power tools were so relatively expensive that it was tempting to invest in attachments for the humble power drill. This is now no longer the case, as the price of these tools has plummeted in real terms; the quality of the machines has also increased, mainly due to improvements in technology, manufacturing techniques and materials. They tend to be lighter in weight, better powered and less fatiguing to use.

Belt Sander

The features to look for are the width of the belt, the speed, and the power of the motor. Widths range from 2in (51mm) on DIY models to about 4in (102mm) on professional hand-held machines. The average length of the sanding area is about 6in (152mm). The width and speed also determine the power of the motor needed to drive it. Obviously, the wider the belt, the

greater the area in contact with the substrate, and the greater the frictional force. A more powerful motor will be needed to overcome this force and drive the belt around without strain and at a good speed. The problem then becomes that of weight. A good compromise is a machine with a 3in (76mm) belt. Belt speeds vary from about 300 metres to about 500 metres per minute.

The depth of cut can be controlled with a sanding frame fixed to the base of the sander, which may be adjusted to vary the cut. It also increases the area of the base overall, and thus helps to keep a flat surface.

Another useful controlling device is variable speed: for a relatively modest additional cost, machines with electronic speed control can increase the versatility of the machine. However, it is not essential in a belt sander, and so can be treated as a luxurious option.

Orbital Sanders

Put simply, the faster the speed of the orbital action, the finer the finish that will be achieved. Again, electronic speed controls are available on some models, though this is not usually needed. The average orbital speed is in the order of 4000–5000 orbits per minute, but the more expensive machines can take this up into five figures.

These sanders are the genuine article when determining what is a finishing power tool. If very fine grades of abrasive are used, i.e. 240 (*see* Chapter 4), exceptionally fine surfaces can be obtained on suitable substrates. In fact, this machine can be used to denib between coats of varnish or lacquer (but *not* French polish).

Orbital sanders are sized according to the area of the sanding base. They come in three basic sizes: third sheet, half sheet and quarter sheet. These sizes refer to the proportion of a standard sheet of abrasive paper 11in × 9in (27.9cm × 22.9cm) to be fitted. A half sheet machine is the best choice for most purposes, while the quarter sheet models are the palm sanders.

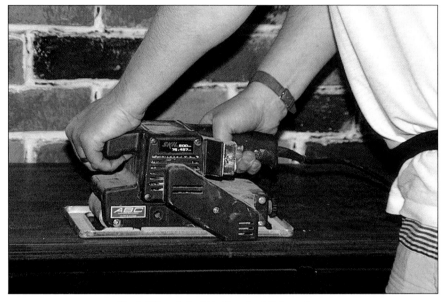

Fig 2.8 How to hold belt and orbital sanders.

SAFETY

A sanding machine should be switched on before being presented to the surface. Starting it up while it is in contact will create a dangerous torque that can wrench the machine from your grip and conceivably cause you or someone nearby an injury – or even damage the work! It should also be lifted from the surface before being switched off. Most machines have a button which, when depressed, keeps the motor running without using the trigger switch. This does have obvious advantages in that it prevents hand fatigue during periods of extended operation, but, while I am an enthusiastic user of this

button, there is one reservation which you should be aware of: what happens if, for some reason, you lose your grip on the machine? This has happened to me, and the sight of a machine pirouetting away beyond my reach, to wreak damage elsewhere, is not to be repeated. The trigger switch doubles up as a 'dead man's switch' – let go, and the machine's motor dies.

The way these machines are held during operation is particularly important: you must keep control at all times. Fig 2.8 shows how both hands are used to maintain the sanding area in contact with the surface. Particular care needs to be taken when the machine reaches the ends and edges, to prevent it from dropping over. Fig 2.9 shows how the pressure applied by

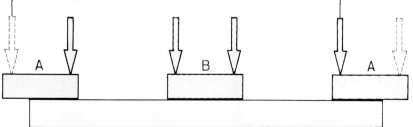

Fig 2.9 Transferring pressure from one hand to the other as the sander approaches the ends of the work.

the hands, light though it is, becomes transferred from one hand to the other as the sander reaches the ends. The positioning of the hands in Fig 2.8 is the same for orbital sanders (except palm sanders, of course, which are operated with one hand only).

There are two other areas of concern when using machinery of this type: electrical safety, and dust and noise.

Electrical safety is much less of a concern these days than it once was, as safety standards dictate that machines are double insulated and that the power and the operator are kept well apart. The cases of hand power tools are now plastic, which affords additional protection. Even so, common sense dictates that they must not be used where water is likely to come into contact with them. In addition, an operator can become so immersed in the job that it is quite easy to snag the cable with the abrasive, and so a circuit breaker also makes sense.

What causes great concern, though, is pollution – both noise and dust. The effect of noise cannot be ignored; it is cumulative and generally irreversible. Many occasions of extended periods of machine noise can damage your hearing, and so the use of a noise attenuator is a must (*see* Fig 2.10). For anyone who has never used one before, they are surprising in the amount of sound that can get through. They reduce the level of machine noise without deafening you to other sounds, and you can hold a perfectly intelligible conversation while still wearing an attenuator.

The effect of dust is also cumulative in its damage effect upon the lungs. Always wear a mask and eyeshields (in case anything is thrown up by the machine). *See* Chapter 3 for more on health and safety.

PHOTOGRAPH COURTESY OF ARCO LTD.

Fig 2.10 A noise attenuator.

Health and
Safety

PHOTOGRAPH COURTESY OF
RACAL SAFETY LTD.

S ome years ago, one of my students was forced to give up her course because of respiratory problems. She was not normally an unhealthy person, nor was there any family history of such disorders. The problem was that every time she used any solvent-based materials, her respiratory tract became so irritated that she found it uncomfortable and distressing to continue working. Even paint, which is not particularly volatile, could not be used without wearing a cartridge respirator.

This illustrates the point that, as individuals, we possess tolerance thresholds that are peculiar to us, and we can often only determine those thresholds through experience. Unfortunately, such experiences can prove very damaging to health and, what is worse, we may not know it is happening until after it is too late. Quite a few occupational diseases only manifest themselves after many years of constant exposure to the materials that are their cause.

The romantic figure of the French polisher huddled over some gleaming piece of furniture, lovingly caressing it with gently curving sweeps of his polish-filled pad, still figures very strongly in the minds of many people. This ideal evokes images of contentment, harmony and pride in craftsmanship, and those people of an age where they can remember craftsmen working in this way may even recall the atmosphere and smells in those workshops. While the traditional French polisher is still alive and kicking, the nature of woodfinishing has changed beyond all recognition over the past four decades or so. No longer are we dealing simply with beeswax and turpentine, linseed oil, alcohol and shellac in French polish, and other such goodies; there are now some very nasty substances, products of the petrochemical industry, that have been produced to answer the call for cost-efficient coatings with improved mechanical properties.

The irony is that while we apply these substances to protect the surface of wood, the woodfinisher frequently needs to cover him- or herself in something for protection against the substances.

It is the mark of a civilized society that we believe in protecting citizens from the harmful activities of other people or from the dangers posed by the results of those activities. As far as the woodfinisher is concerned, the two most important pieces of legislation that affect his or her working life are the Health and Safety at Work Act 1974, and the Control of Substances Hazardous to Health (COSHH) Regulations 1988. To these two cornerstones must be added specific legislation governing the use of particular materials.

HEALTH AND SAFETY AT WORK ACT 1974, AND COSHH

It is not my intention to discuss these laws and regulations in detail, as this is not really within the scope of woodfinishing. However, they are of such importance that any book on the subject must address the issue, if only to raise awareness of their existence and importance. Anyone wishing to pursue more detailed knowledge should contact their local Environmental Health Department or regional office of the Health and Safety Executive.

Essentially, the Health and Safety Act is a piece of umbrella legislation, not only providing protection under the terms as originally drawn up in the early 1970s, but also empowering the Health and Safety Executive, through the government of the day, to introduce regulations that strengthen the law. One of the most important of these sets of regulations is the Control of Substances Hazardous to Health Regulations 1988 (COSHH). These regulations came into effect in October 1989, and are a very powerful addition to the law.

One of the main strengths of the COSHH regulations is the way in which they have involved everyone in a firm in the process of identifying potentially harmful substances in their working environment and in producing strategies to minimize risk, as well as continuously monitoring the use of hazardous materials. Under the terms of COSHH, all substances that have any potential to harm (as far as such knowledge is available) have to be identified and recorded. For each of these substances a code of practice has to be drawn up, to protect people from levels of exposure considered harmful.

The values attached to these limits are referred to as Occupational Exposure Limits (OEL). Each identified hazardous substance has its own OEL (expressed as parts per million or milligrams per cubic metre), and this can be found in the Health and Safety Executive Guidance Notes EH/40, obtainable from the Health and Safety Executive (HSE). These notes are issued annually, revised to reflect current wisdom. A list of HSE Guidance Notes relevant to the woodfinisher is given on page 31.

OELs are further classified according to whether they are Controlled or Recommended: Controlled limits should not be exceeded, while Recommended limits are considered good practice. The values are also expressed as long- and short-term limits. A long-term limit is the average exposure concentration over an eight-hour period (referred to as eight-hour time weighted average), while the short-term limit relates to the maximum concentration an operator might be exposed to over any single 10-minute period (referred to as the 10-minute time weighted average). Remember that inhalation is not the only form of exposure: ingestion (especially while eating or drinking) is a common form of exposure, and absorption through bare skin is another.

If you are an individual craftsman, possibly an amateur, or maybe a young professional about to start up on your own, you may feel that such regulations will have little relevance to you.

After all, how can you measure such things, and as an individual craftsman not employing anyone, you don't really fall within the scope of these regulations. I feel compelled to caution against such a view, as COSHH has at least two effects that have far-reaching consequences.

The obligation to examine closely the possible effects of all materials you use cannot be a bad thing at all; it is far too easy to be laid-back about the whole issue. The second consequence is more long-term in that, having looked at what you use and the difficulties some of those materials pose, is it better to use something else instead? If it is going to become expensive or incredibly inconvenient to render harmful and toxic materials impotent, is it more cost-effective in the long term to produce a 'harmless' alternative?

A considerable amount of money is being spent by companies on research and development in the search for products that are based on less harmful materials, which yet retain similar characteristics (and better ones, if possible) to those they are replacing. For example, we have seen the introduction of water-based varnishes which have many of the useful properties of the oil- and solvent-based products; they are also faster drying, which allows three coats to be applied in one day, and the equipment can be cleaned in water.

CLASSIFICATION, PACKAGING AND LABELLING OF DANGEROUS SUBSTANCES REGULATIONS (1984)

Fig 3.1 shows an example of a container label providing information aimed at warning the user of the hazards associated with the product. This is now a legal requirement on all containers holding hazardous materials sold to the public (whether a professional user or not). The format of such a supply label as laid down by the CPL Regulations are as follows:

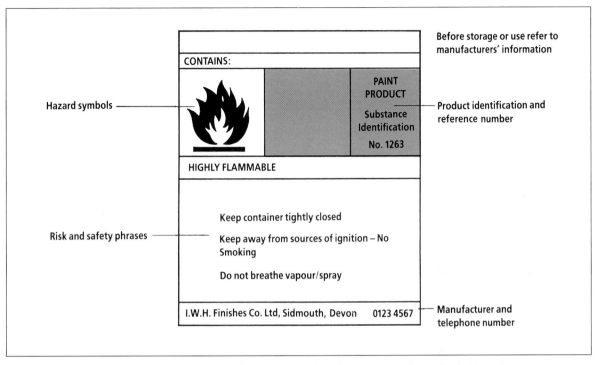

Hazard symbols

Risk and safety phrases

CONTAINS:

PAINT PRODUCT

Substance Identification No. 1263

HIGHLY FLAMMABLE

Keep container tightly closed

Keep away from sources of ignition – No Smoking

Do not breathe vapour/spray

I.W.H. Finishes Co. Ltd, Sidmouth, Devon   0123 4567

Before storage or use refer to manufacturers' information

Product identification and reference number

Manufacturer and telephone number

Fig 3.1 Container labelling conforming to the Classification, Packaging and Labelling of Dangerous Substances Regulations 1984.

Product and Reference Number

These are specific to the company supplying the product, and are a quick and obvious means of identification.

Hazardous Substances

The label must name the substances that pose a hazard.

Substance Identification No. (UN Number)

This is a number that is unique to the hazardous substance and acts as another means of identifying it.

Hazard Symbols

There are six basic symbols used to indicate the general nature of the hazard. This immediate recognition of hazard is a ready means of enabling handlers of the product to adopt

appropriate procedures. Symbols are also quicker to recognize than lines of text – another quick way of alerting attention to a potential problem.

Risk and Safety Phrases

These are used to indicate the risks to health that exposure to the substance presents (risk phrases), and to advise on how these risks can be avoided (safety phrases). Up to four risk and four safety phrases may be used; any more would reduce the impact of the information, because the label is intended to give quick identification of the product and its associated risks.

Manufacturer/Supplier

Should the need arise, this information is present so that the company can be contacted regarding any difficulties and at the same time be held accountable.

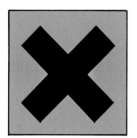

Toxic

Harmful

Corrosive

Irritant

Highly flammable

Oxidizing

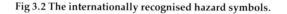

Fig 3.2 The internationally recognised hazard symbols.

HAZARD SYMBOLS

Fig 3.2 shows the internationally recognized hazard symbols that by law must be used on packaging containing a hazardous substance:

Toxic Where serious, acute and chronic health risks, and possibly death, may be involved.

Harmful Where limited health risks may be involved.

Corrosive Where contact with living tissues may destroy them.

Irritant Where inflammation may be caused following contact with skin or mucous membranes.

Highly flammable Where the product has a flash point below 22°C.

Oxidizing Where oxygen is released during a chemical reaction.

These symbols can be used in combination with each other when more than one hazard is involved, i.e. hydrogen peroxide is used as a wood bleach and reacts with any alkaline substance to release chemically active oxygen. This may make it a slight fire risk (although it is not flammable in its own right), but more importantly, it is corrosive if it comes into contact with your skin. The oxidizing and corrosive symbols would therefore be found together on the packaging.

Manufacturers have to provide comprehensive Health and Safety Data notes for each hazardous product they supply. Apart from a comprehensive description of the hazardous nature of the product, the notes will also include such things as what precautions should be taken during use, what first aid should be administered in the case of an operator suffering from the effects of exposure, fire prevention, and disposal of the product if it is no longer needed or goes beyond its usable lifespan. If you buy such a product, ask for the notes, which will be supplied free.

SPRAYING – PROTECTIVE CLOTHING

A finely atomized mist is caused by oversprayed lacquer, paint, etc., and this hangs in the air for

a considerable period. Additional hazards are created as a result.

Dust

The solvent rapidly evaporates from the atomized materials – within seconds if the workshop is warm – leaving a 'mist' of solid particles. This dust will remain in the air for a long time, and will present a potential health hazard if inhaled, or may irritate the skin and mucous membranes of the respiratory tract or eyes. It is essential that total body protection is achieved to prevent inhalation, ingestion (by swallowing the dust) and contact with skin or clothes. Fig 3.3 is not someone kitted up to enter a nuclear pile, but to spray a noxious lacquer!

The overalls are lightweight and made of paper, and are disposable after one wearing. Gloves protect the hands. The headgear is fed with a continuous supply of clean, filtered air which enters over the top of the head and gently

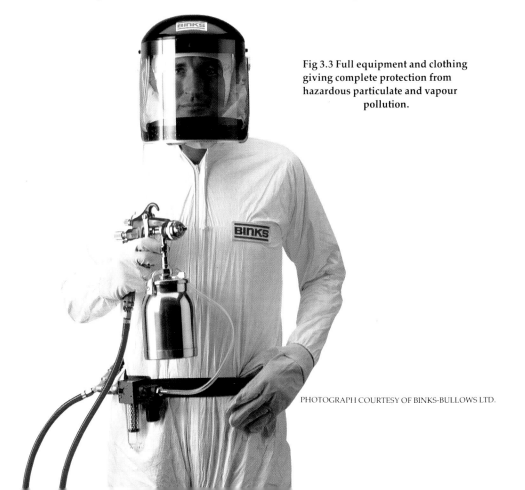

Fig 3.3 Full equipment and clothing giving complete protection from hazardous particulate and vapour pollution.

PHOTOGRAPH COURTESY OF BINKS-BULLOWS LTD.

passes downward over the face, ensuring that any air that may try to enter from the outside is kept out by a tidal stream of fresh air.

This particular system is the top end of the range: the air being fed into the headgear comes from the same airline that feeds the spray equipment (although its pressure is very much reduced). The source of this air is obviously from outside the contaminated area. Cheaper but equally effective head units can be bought, where the air source is the contaminated area and it is filtered before being pumped across the face. These units are battery-operated and, being self-contained, give a considerable degree of freedom to move about.

Vapour

It follows from the above that if solvent rapidly evaporates from the oversprayed material, the air will have a high concentration of solvent vapour in it. The equipment shown in Fig 3.3 will provide total protection from exposure. The self-contained, battery-operated mask will need to be fitted with a filter that will absorb the vapour; the literature provided with the mask will give information about the types of filter that can be supplied to fit the equipment.

If you are a lone craftsman working on a very tight budget, you may not be willing or really able to invest in this expensive equipment; it is possible to buy eye protectors and respirator masks that still conform to British Standards specifications. Fig 3.4 shows one such respirator: it simply covers the mouth and nose, and so offers no protection for your skin or eyes. It is therefore not suitable for use where the manufacturer indicates that a material can enter your body through the skin. This information will be given in the firm's Health and Safety Data notes for that particular product.

Flammability of this vapour is a major concern. When woodfinishing solvents evaporate, they form a mixture with the air which is potentially explosive. The actual concentration at which this occurs varies with each solvent, but an indication of flammability is given by the flash point: this is the temperature at which the vapour can form a

Fig 3.4 A low-cost respirator with appropriate gas cartridge, conforming to the relevant British Standard.

flammable mixture with the air. The lower the flash point, the greater the flammability.

Most spray materials have a flash point below 22°C, and this classifies them as highly flammable. Refer to the Health and Safety literature listed below for further information on handling, storing and using these materials.

SPRAYING – EXTRACTION SYSTEMS

The safest way to use sprayed materials is with some form of safe extraction system. The most common way of doing this is by using a spray booth. There are two basic types: dry back and water-washed, and they are described in detail in Chapter 9.

The main advantage of a spray booth is that overspray and solvent vapour are restricted to a very small area, and their removal ensures a safe environment. The spray operator also benefits because overspray is drawn away from him or her.

WOODFINISHING AND STATUTORY REGULATIONS

Copies of these Regulations and Acts of Parliament may be obtained from HMSO:

The Factories Act 1961
The Protection of Eyes Regulations 1974
The Petroleum (Consolidation) Act 1928
The Petroleum (Mixtures) Order 1929
The Highly Flammable Liquids and
    Liquefied Petroleum Gases
    Regulations 1972
The Control of Pollution Act 1974
Control of Lead at Work Regulations 1980
Control of Pollution (Special Waste)
    Regulations 1980

Health and Safety at Work etc. Act 1974
Consumer Protection Act 1987
Classification, Packaging and Labelling of
    Dangerous Substances Regulations 1984
The Control of Pollution (Collection and Disposal of Waste) Regulations 1988
Control of Substances Hazardous to Health
    Regulations 1988

These govern the use of many of the materials used in woodfinishing, but the legalistic nature of the documents does not make them particularly user-friendly. The Health and Safety Executive produce a range of guides that explain the obligations and responsibilities in a way that is comprehensible. Among them are:

CS/2 The Storage of Highly Flammable Liquids
EH/5 Trichloroethylene: Health and Safety Precautions
EH/9 Spraying of Highly Flammable Liquids
EH/16 Isocyanates – Toxic Hazards and Precautions
EH/40 Occupational Exposure Limits
EH/42 Monitoring Strategies for Toxic Substances
EH/44 Dust in the Workplace
HS(G)4 Highly Flammable Liquids in the Paint Industry
HS(G)27 Substances for Use at Work – the Provision of Information
HS(R)22 Guide to the Classification, Packaging and Labelling of Dangerous Substances Regulations 1984
HS(R) Guide to Highly Flammable Liquids and Liquefied Petroleum Gases Regulations 1972

There are also standards for safety equipment:

Specification for Industrial Eye Protectors, BS2092 1967
Selection, Use and Maintenance of Respiratory Protective Equipment, BS4275 1968
Specification for Respirators for Protection Against Harmful Dusts and Gases, BS2091
Breathing Apparatus, BS4667 1974

Surface
Preparation

A great deal will be made of meticulous attention to detail in applying the range of finishes described in this book, but it must never be forgotten that, no matter how much care you take in applying polish, if the wood surface itself is not adequately prepared to receive it, the end result will be, at the very least, disappointing.

The reason for this is that a finish not only protects the wood surface, but also highlights any blemishes on it. This is particularly true of the gloss finishes: French polishing, for instance, quickly shows up any deficiencies in craftsman-ship – its mirror-like lustre can only be achieved on a perfectly smooth ground, and even the slightest blemish will ruin the effect.

A brief explanation of optics will help to illus-trate the effect. A smooth polished surface acts as a mirror, reflecting light to our eyes so that we see a reflection of objects (*see* Fig 4.1). Fig 4.2 illustrates the effect of a blemish, in this case a small planing tear in the surface fibres of the wood. In effect, the blemish creates many different reflective surfaces, all at different angles to each other, and each reflects light in a different direction. The result is that the blemish

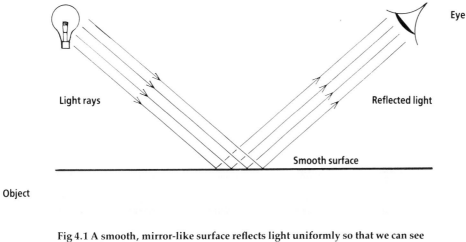

Fig 4.1 A smooth, mirror-like surface reflects light uniformly so that we can see perfect reflections of objects placed in front.

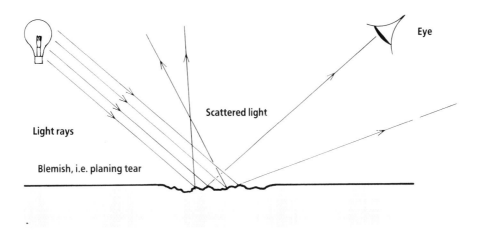

Fig 4.2 Blemishes, such as planing tears, will scatter light in all directions, making the area appear darker and duller because less light reaches our eyes.

scatters light and so produces a break in the otherwise perfect reflection from the rest of the surface. The problem is that sometimes these blemishes do not appear to exist until you start applying the finish, at which point they reveal themselves in a manner that makes you believe that the whole thing was a conspiracy to catch you out. In fact, the unpolished surface is not usually a good reflector of light, so you do not always notice these tiny blemishes. However, they cannot escape your sense of touch, so during the process of preparing the surface, slowly run your fingers over the work without applying any pressure, and also put your eye level pretty close to that of the surface (*see* Fig 4.3), as looking obliquely at a low angle is more revealing than looking from directly above. The combination of sight and touch is formidable.

There is a fairly widespread misconception that a surface defect can somehow be masked with stain and polish, as if to 'paint' it out. While there certainly is a technique used by professional polishers to mask certain blemishes, it is generally untrue that you can paper over the cracks – they need to be repaired.

SMOOTHING TOOLS

It is rare for a piece of wood to be smooth enough to polish direct from a plane iron. There are usually a number of marks caused by the plane, such as tears or undulations (due to the curved nature of jack and fore plane irons), or the occasional ridge caused by a chip in the edge of the iron. Machine-planed timber is even less likely to be suitable for polishing direct from the knives (*see* Fig 4.4).

Bruises, marking knife lines and pencil marks (not to mention grime caused by constant handling) need to be removed: this can be done with abrasive papers, but would take a long time.

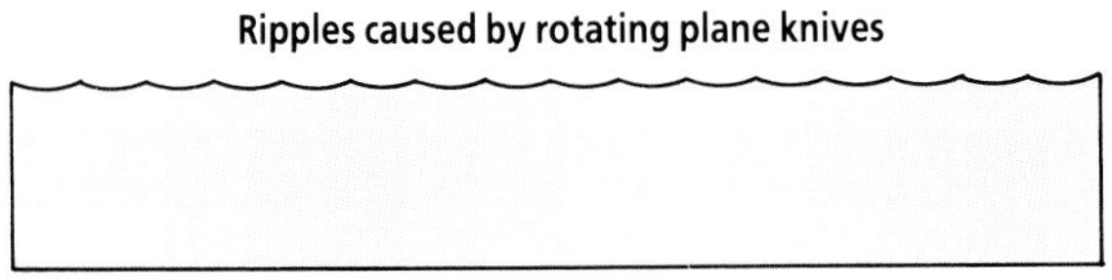

Ripples caused by rotating plane knives

Fig 4.4 Exaggerated view of rippled effect sometimes caused by machine planing.

Fig 4.3 Examining a surface against the light to find blemishes.

There are two tools made for the job of cleaning up the work prior to staining and polishing:

Smoothing Plane

The iron should be extremely sharp and set very fine, to take shavings so thin as to be almost transparent. The edge of the iron should be perfectly square, with the ends slightly rounded to prevent them digging in.

On difficult timbers, where the grain is running in more than one direction, you must take extra care not to plane against the grain. This might mean changing the direction of planing to minimize the amount of tearing. Fig 4.5 shows typical grain configurations and how

to plane them. Incidentally, a test of skill in the use of a plane is to prepare a piece of wood so that it is ready to polish straight from the smoothing plane.

Cabinet Scraper

This simple, but extremely effective, tool seems to cause problems out of all proportion to its simplicity. Despite its name, it is a cutting, not a scraping, tool. It must produce tiny shavings, not all dust. It is made of tool steel and is thin enough to be flexible, but hard enough to take a burr on its long edges. Cabinet scrapers can be bought in a variety of sizes and shapes. Fig 4.6 shows the basic shapes: for flat surfaces; 'goose-necked' for hollows of various radii; with one end for convex surfaces and the other for shallow hollows. The latter two are clearly used for parts that a smoothing plane cannot reach.

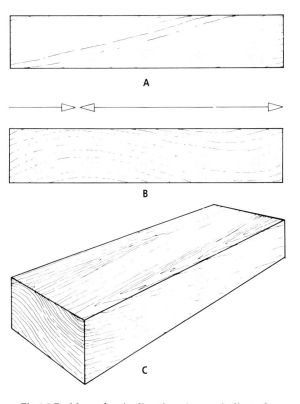

Fig 4.5 Problem of grain direction. Arrows indicate the planing direction. With (c), some tearing out is inevitable, in whatever direction you plane; (a) no problem in planing; (b) wavy grain; (c) grain direction alternates in streaks across the width of the wood.

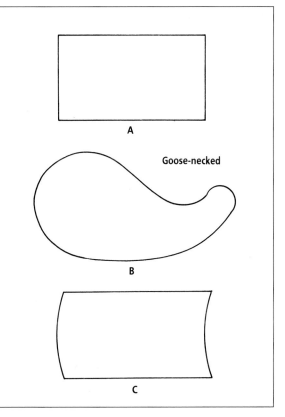

Fig 4.6 Cabinet scraper shapes.

SHARPENING A SCRAPER

Over the years, literally thousands upon thousands of words describing the method of preparing a scraper have appeared, each description being different in some respects – so the picture becomes a little confusing. Sharpening this tool is a knack which is not difficult to achieve, provided you understand the basic principle behind the technique. In essence, you are producing an edge which is straight, square across its width and burnished smooth of any marks. This edge is then 'turned' to produce a burr, which is what actually cuts the wood.

Even a brand-new scraper needs to be sharpened. Hold it in a vice with a long edge horizontal; with a fine metal file, produce a

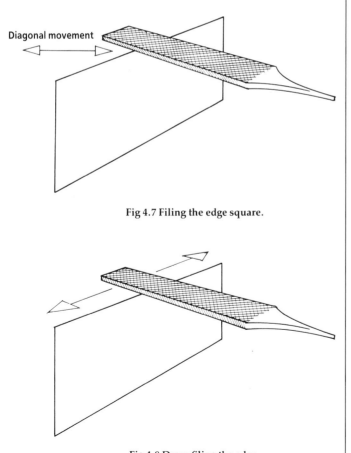

Fig 4.7 Filing the edge square.

Fig 4.8 Draw-filing the edge.

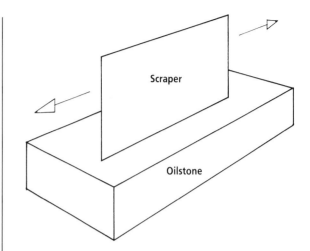

Fig 4.9 Burnishing edge on fine stone.

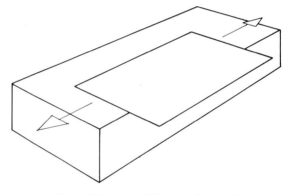

Fig 4.10 Removing filing burr from side.

straight edge which is square across (*see* Fig 4.7), then draw-file to remove marks made by the teeth (*see* Fig 4.8). The edge is now rubbed on a fine oil- or water stone to remove all traces of file marks (*see* Fig 4.9). There will now be a rough burr on the edge, which is levelled off by rubbing the sides of the scraper on the stone (*see* Fig 4.10); this procedure is repeated on the other long edge.

A new burr must be made, using a 'burnisher' made of high-speed steel rod (¼in–⅜in dia.), mounted in a wooden handle. The rod is held horizontal and drawn hard along each long edge once. It is then drawn along it depressed about 5° from the horizontal on both sides of the edge, to produce the burr. Repeat on the other long edge (*see* Fig 4.11), and the new scraper is now ready for use. For future sharpening, the four old burrs need to be removed first, by honing the flat faces on the fine stone.

The shaped scrapers cannot be sharpened this way; old burrs are removed by honing and the edge is burnished ready for turning, using fine carborundum paper wrapped around a wooden dowel. The edges are turned in the same manner with the burnisher.

USING THE SCRAPER

Hold the scraper as shown in Fig 4.12, with both thumbs flexing the centre and the fingers of both hands curled around the short edges to support it. Push the blade along the surface, tilted just off the vertical so that the burr cuts. A guillotining action is needed, with the blade set slightly skew to the direction of cut, which should always be along the grain. This eases the cutting action, but also means that some of the blade will be on the wood at the ends of the stroke so it is supported and the edge of the wood is not damaged by the scraper falling off.

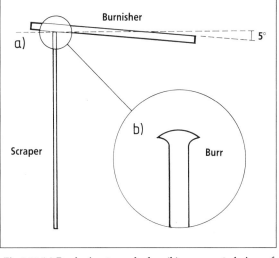

Fig 4.11 (a) Producing turned edge; (b) exaggerated view of the edge.

If the scraper has been correctly sharpened, very fine shavings will be produced, and, on very hard woods, the surface will take on a sheen as it is smoothed. For very difficult grain configurations, a scraper is an alternative to the smoothing plane, as it does not tear out the fibres. In all other cases, it is used after the plane. Always take long strokes from one end of the

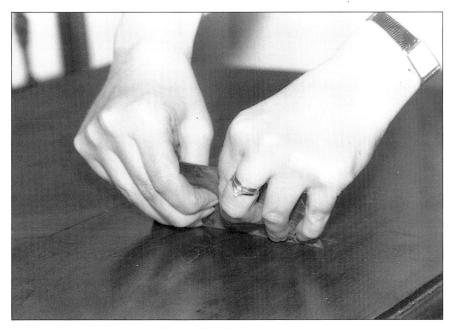

Fig 4.12 Holding the scraper.

wood to the other if possible, to prevent hollowing of the surface and reduce the risk of marking. The scraper can get very hot, and will burn your thumbs, so wear sticking plasters to protect them.

ABRASIVES

On the back of abrasive paper you will see numbers and codes, which refer to the coarseness of the abrasive; the important number is the grit size, as this is the only number which is consistent across the different brands. The higher the number, the finer the particles. For the finisher, the important grit sizes range from 150, for initial preparation, through to 320, for ultra-smooth surfaces ready for polishing. The number actually represents the size of the particles that can pass through a mesh whose holes per square centimetre correspond to the grit number: a paper which gives a grit size of 240 has particles that can pass through a mesh with 240 holes per square centimetre.

Abrasive papers come in two main weights, A and C: A weight paper is fairly lightweight, with closely spaced particles and thin backing

paper, and is designed for hand sanding. C weight is heavier-duty, with a thick backing paper and particles that are further apart. Such papers are sometimes called open-coat. They are designed for use on sanding machines, hence their toughness. As a machine will obviously move the paper at a much faster speed than the human hand, the wider spacings of the particles are needed to reduce clogging. In general, C weight papers do not come in the finer grits, and A weight papers are not often to be found in the very coarse grits.

There are a number of different types of abrasive papers in common use:

Glasspaper

Particles of ground glass are bonded on to the paper. This is not a very good abrasive, as the particles quickly lose their edge.

Garnet Paper

Ground garnet stone is the abrasive. This is a long-lasting paper, and represents very good value for money. It has a good cut on bare and polished wood, making it suitable for initial preparation of the surface and for cutting back the first coat or two of polish.

Aluminium Oxide

Also called production paper, this mineral is hard enough to use on metal. Again, it is very long-lasting and good value for money.

Silicon Carbide

The hardest of the common abrasive papers, this comes in a waterproof version which everyone knows as wet-or-dry. It is a very expensive paper, but is obtainable in grit sizes down to 1200, very useful for cutting back rubber burns during French polishing. The 600 grit, used wet,

GRIT SIZE	GLASSPAPER CODES	GRADE
320	—	9/0
280	—	8/0
240	—	7/0
220	00	6/0
150	0	4/0
120	1	3/0
100	1½	2/0
80	F2	0
60	M2	½
50	S2	1
30	2½	1½
24	3	2

Table 2 Comparison of abrasive grading codes appropriate for woodfinishing.

is ideal for rubbing down between coats of French polish, polyurethane or yacht varnish, to produce a very fine finish.

Lubrisil

Silicon carbide again, but this paper contains its own lubricant that helps to prevent clogging. It is a great favourite of many woodturners, as its resistance to clogging makes it ideal for high-speed sanding. It is a matter of personal preference, of course, but I have not found its expense justified by its performance, and tend to stick to garnet, production and wet-or-dry.

Nylon Mesh Abrasive Pads

A recent innovation is the appearance of nylon mesh pads impregnated with abrasive material. The grades available are purely descriptive, i.e. coarse, fine and ultra-fine. The ultra-fine grade is extremely useful for smoothing between coats of French polish and spray lacquers.

PREPARING A SURFACE

The nature of the surface will to a large degree determine the best method of smoothing. For a better understanding of this, three broad categories of surface are identified below:

New, Solid Wood

Use a smoothing plane initially, and then finish off with the cabinet scraper. It has to be said that the scraper is not much use on softwoods, as the softness of the fibres make the surface spring under the pressure of the scraper, and virtually no cutting takes place. So only use the scraper on hardwoods.

For coarse-grained timbers such as oak and ash, which are to be waxed or oiled, the surface is usually quite all right to take the polish direct

from the scraper blade, as it allows for a certain rustic charm. For any other finish, such timbers must be sanded.

If a scraper has not been used, begin with a grit size of 150; always sand with the grain and never across it, as cross-sanding always leaves scratches which show through the polish. This means extra care when sanding panelled work where adjoining members have different grain directions (i.e. rails and stiles). Fig 4.13 shows the order of sanding the members of panelled work; any accidental cross-sanding at the joints will be eliminated later on.

Dust off regularly, and when the paper seems to be gliding over the surface, it is time to change to a finer grit and repeat the process. Each grade leaves its own tiny scratches, and by passing to progressively finer grit sizes they become less: move from 150 to 180, and then 240 grits. If the wood is particularly fine-grained (e.g. sycamore or satinwood) or you are French polishing the work, finish off with 320 grit. By the time you

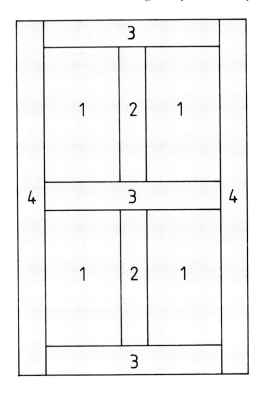

Fig 4.13 Order in sanding panelled work.

have finished, the wood should have a definite sheen if it is smooth enough.

Always use a cork rubber on large flat surfaces, and never dwell on any one area; rather, take long strokes and work the whole surface once, and come back to start again. This way you will prevent localized hollows.

Mouldings can present a problem, as their profiles are often rapidly destroyed by careless use of the paper. Either use a sanding block of the reverse profile, or use nylon mesh abrasive, which moulds itself to the profile.

Veneered Work

Veneers are thin, making it easy to sand straight through to the groundwork beneath. Clearly, you cannot use very coarse abrasives, and there should be no need for them anyway, as the surface will be relatively smooth. Use a 240 grit, quickly followed by 320.

Marquetry, quartered and inlaid work will have grain running in different directions. It is not feasible to keep changing the direction of sanding, so start with 240 grit to reduce the risk of obvious cross-sanding marks showing through the final polish. Yet another problem can occur when dark and light veneers are used: the grain of the light veneer tends to turn dark as dust from the dark veneer is forced in. Regularly dust down, and when you have finished, a blast of compressed air will clear out the grain. Under no circumstances use a damp rag, as this will fix the dust in the grain.

Stripped Surfaces

These have already been through the stage of surface preparation before receiving the finish that has just been stripped. They are, therefore, different to new surfaces in a number of respects.

First, they will be smoother, so a fine grit such as 240 or 320 should be quite sufficient, even if water has been used in the stripping process as

a neutralizer, making the wood a little fuzzy. Use a minimum of sanding.

Second, veneers may present a couple of problems: there may be bubbles, or lifting edges and veneer joints. These should be dealt with before continuing.

Third, during its life, the wood may have acquired scratches and dents. You have to decide whether or not you can live with them. In my view, unless they are disfiguring or will prevent you attaining the finish you require, then leave them. There is little point using filler in very shallow depressions, as it is always detectable (and may look worse than the damage) and will probably fall out anyway. Shallow dents can be steamed out as described below.

MACHINE SANDING

Chapter 2 deals with sanding machines suitable for use in producing a fine finish prior to staining and polishing, and here we look at the situations in which it is acceptable to use such machines.

Belt sanders are to be used for preliminary sanding, and must never be used on thin veneers. They have no place in refinishing work where the surface is pretty smooth to begin with. They are at their best if used directly from planing, either by hand or machine; in fact, if a machine planer has left the sort of ripples shown in Fig 4.4, a smoothing plane is really the best way of beginning to tackle the problem, unless you have access to industrial table belt sanders.

The hand planing can be followed by the use of a cabinet scraper, then the sander, using a belt with 120 grit or thereabouts. The result should be a surface that is level and uniform. If there are any tears in the wood, the best way of removing them is with a smooth plane, cabinet scraper or by filling (*see* below).

An orbital sander can be used for the final sanding, working through the finer grits as already described. Begin with a 180 grit followed by 240, dusting off the work regularly, otherwise unsightly scratching can occur.

Given the obvious advantages of machine sanding, there is still the need for a visual inspection and the use of hand sanding for localized problem areas. To the purist (or masochist, depending on your point of view), hand sanding cannot be replaced if the ultimate in surface preparation is required.

FINAL PREPARATIONS

If a water-based stain is to be used, the surface needs to be moistened with warm water and allowed to dry, to forestall any tendency for the stain to swell the fibres of the wood. By wetting at this stage, allowing the fibres to swell, and then sanding with a 320 grit paper, there will be little or no swelling after applying the stain, when you would be unable to cut back the raised fibre, at least not without making the stain very patchy.

Despite the warnings above about the use of fillers, there may be blemishes that need to be filled. The material used as a filler will depend on the finish you intend to use. If the wood is to be waxed, use a coloured wax stick, which you can make yourself (*see* Chapter 16). The wax is melted into the blemish using the tang of a file heated by a spirit burner (*see* Fig 4.14). For French polish a shellac stick is melted into the blemish in a similar way. In both cases, the sticks are made in a range of colours to match that of the stained surface, and the blemish is filled proud of the surface; when it has hardened, the filler is levelled with a sharp chisel. Proprietary stoppers can be bought for most other finishes. Wax and shellac stopping are often referred to as beaumontage.

You may prefer to carry out this filling stage after staining, when it will be easier to match the colour to the stain; this is fine, but take care when levelling, as it is too easy to cut through the stain.

Minor depressions that are too shallow to fill (the beaumontage will fall out) can usually be steamed out before staining. Place a clean wet cloth over the patch and press a hot clothes iron on to it; the steam generated will be forced into the compressed fibres, causing them to swell. Two or three attempts may be needed. Afterwards, when the area has dried, smooth with fine abrasive paper.

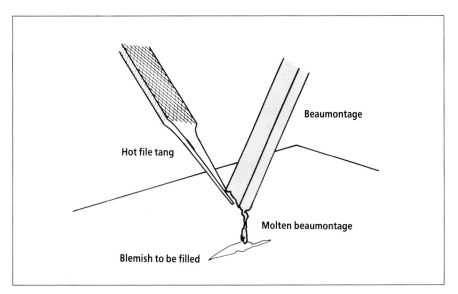

Fig 4.14 Melting beaumontage into a deep blemish.

Hot file tang

Beaumontage

Molten beaumontage

Blemish to be filled

Staining
and
Bleaching

PHOTOGRAPH COURTESY OF CUPRINOL LTD.

There are still some suspicions surrounding the use of staining materials in woodworking – in a few cases, people still believe you are trying to hide something! In the vast majority of instances, however, it is a matter of fashion, taste or plain convention. I shall restrict explanations to the more prosaic and most frequent reasons for wanting to change the natural colour of wood.

CHANGING THE COLOUR

Disguising inferior wood to make it appear rather better is an obvious reason, but since this is not good craftsmanship, I shall diplomatically ignore it. The following are, in my view, legitimate reasons for wanting to change wood colour.

Uniformity As it is a natural material, wood will exhibit variations in colour, texture and the like, and this is part of its charm. It can also cause a problem in that wood used from different sources, or even different parts of the same tree, may vary in colour to a significant degree. This may not suit your purpose, so staining or bleaching is a legitimate means of gaining uniformity.

Disguise This is probably an unfortunate word because of its connotations; what I really mean is that you may wish to make a perfectly good piece of wood resemble a different species. There is absolutely nothing wrong with this; for example, beech is the ideal wood for chair frames and other similar articles that require considerable structural strength. It is hard, very close-grained and incredibly boring to look at. By staining it to resemble mahogany, walnut, oak, etc., you are making it more interesting to view.

Matching and blending This is probably the most difficult of colouring tasks. New wood used in a repair will need to be coloured to match that which surrounds it, or a new piece of furniture or a built-in must be coloured to blend in with other items of furniture or a general colour scheme.

Protection In Chapter 12, the use of preservative materials will be discussed in detail. The one thing common to all those designed for exterior use is that they are heavily coloured with special chemicals that protect the wood from the considerable damaging effects of ultraviolet (UV) light from the sun. A clear preservative will protect timbers from fungal and insect attack, but never underestimate the effects of the sun: those timbers would quickly disintegrate as the fibres broke down, due to the chemical effect of UV on organic material.

STAINING MATERIALS

In theory, any coloured material could be employed to stain wood, and there are a number of exotic examples used in the furniture restoration trade. It is probably wise to indicate at this stage that the choice of staining material may be determined by the finish you intend to employ; in certain circumstances, the finish may be incompatible with the stain.

The staining material may also be included in the finish itself, such as polyurethane stain varnish. The advantage lies in that the staining process is not needed, and so such a material saves time. It also produces a more even colour on pine, which tends to absorb normal stains unevenly. In commercial finishing, the lacquer itself is coloured, which leads to the irritating effect of light areas when the lacquer chips, as the colour lies as a film over the wood, rather than in it. Such varnishes have one other major drawback: because they form a heavily coloured film over the surface, the wood's figure is often masked and, worse still, inlays are effectively lost.

For the home craftsman and the professional polisher not concerned with production techniques, the following staining materials, along with their characteristics and pitfalls, are those most likely to be encountered. Anyone concerned or interested in the use of synthetic lacquers will find information on stains for use with them, although it is worth noting at this point that water-based stains are generally compatible with all finishing materials.

Oil Stains

Still by far the most commonly used product, these are based on white spirit as the solvent, with a binder to hold the colour in the wood once the solvent has dried. In effect, they are very weak varnishes. This means only one coat should be used, for two reasons:

▌ Successive coats produce a surface film which looks varnished.

▌ You run the risk of dissolving the binder and lifting the colour out of the wood, again creating a patchy effect (this is especially the case if insufficient drying time has been given).

Having said that, oil stains have some extremely attractive features, which is why they are a commercial success in the DIY market. First, they are relatively easy to use, producing a generally uniform colour. They have good penetration and coverage, but are expensive. They are designed to be applied by brush or pad. Everyone has used them at some time or other, and the typical brand names of Colron, Blackfriars and Rustin's will immediately be familiar.

The other great thing about them is that they are produced in standard colours, like paint, and each brand name has its own colour chart; go carefully, however, as the samples are usually on plywood or pine, which is initially white. You must always take into account (with all stains, in fact) that the final colour will be modified by that of the wood, i.e. you may find that a 'walnut' stain looks better on mahogany than a 'mahogany' stain. There is a general rule of thumb in staining: test the colour first on a scrap piece of the wood you have used, or in an inconspicuous area.

You can also extend the colour range by mixing different colours, but keep to the same brand as they will not all have the same composition.

During use, it is an advantage to decant stain into a wide-necked container. Do not use plastic – the solvent dissolves certain plastics, notably margarine tubs and disposable plastic cups.

Possible problems are that polyurethane varnish and wax polish may cause bleeding of the colour by dissolving the binder. It is therefore important to give the work a brush coat of transparent French polish before using wax or varnish to create an isolating film. The same problem will exist if you use cellulose lacquers and cellulose-based sanding sealers.

Acrylic Dyes

These, the latest generation of dyes, are water-based, use an acrylic polymer as the binder, and are ideal for use under the equally new generation of acrylic varnishes. The dyes are fast-drying, have large coverage and generally produce softer colours, which appears to be characteristic of all water-based dyes. Those that use other solvents tend to be brighter or harsher.

As they are based on water, there is the risk of grain raising as described on page 41, but my own, as yet limited, use of these stains indicates that it is not an enormous problem, as they contain an anti-grain-raising ingredient. Again, they are applied by brush or pad and are compatible with all finishes.

Aniline Dyes

Invented in Germany in the nineteenth century, these chemicals, a product of coal tar, produce an enormous range of colours. They are bought in powder form as single colours (e.g. red, blue, green, yellow) or as specific wood colours. There are two varieties: one uses meths as the solvent, the other uses water. The former has little value for the amateur craftsman, as it dries far too quickly, creating tidemarks. However, these dyes can be sprayed on with care, and their bright colours can lead to some exciting effects.

Unfortunately, they fade rather quickly in the presence of strong sunlight. Red is particularly vulnerable, and I have had the experience of a mahogany table stained with spirit dyes that was completely sunbleached in a week! The professional polisher uses them to tint French polish when correcting a colour cast, and for spraying in production work, where a rapid throughput is required. Restorers use them to colour-match new patched pieces to the original material.

The water-based anilines are very useful in that they allow you to make up your own colours, which is ideal for restoring furniture or any other application where the matching up of colours is important.

Both forms are highly soluble in their respective solvents, and are extremely powerful colouring agents. A teaspoon of powder to a pint of solvent will produce quite a strong colour.

If you are mixing your own colour, it is better to make up the solutions and mix them, testing the colour on scrap wood. The depth of colour is controlled, as you might expect, by altering the concentration of the solution. In general, make up strong solutions, mix to the colour you want, and then dilute. Of course, never mix water- and spirit-based dyes.

Water-based anilines are compatible with all finishes and penetrate the wood, but spirit dyes may be lifted by French polish (as it is meths-based). If you use spirit anilines, it will be necessary to add a little transparent French polish as a binder, as they tend not to penetrate but to lie on the surface. If heavily applied, they will mask the wood surface.

Add a dash of ammonia to water anilines, to break down the surface tension of water and so aid penetration of the wood.

Vandyke Crystals

Sometimes referred to as walnut crystals, these are produced by pressing out the juice from unripe walnut shells, the same material added to so-called walnut extract shampoo to enrich the colour of brown hair.

The crystals are water-soluble, and produce a basic chestnut brown traditionally used on walnut and oak. According to concentration, the depth of colour can be varied from honey to black. They do not dissolve easily, and the following method will make the job easier. Mix the crystals to a paste with hot water, and then gradually add more hot water to dissolve. Add a dash of ammonia to aid penetration. Test the colour and adjust the concentration as necessary. Store the stain in a wide-necked jar. As the water cools, some of the crystals come out of solution and form a sediment at the bottom. This sediment can be retrieved later and redissolved in more hot water.

If the solution is very concentrated, the stain has a tendency to be a little sticky during application and to become streaky. The good thing is that it can be washed off with a wet rag, and so colour adjustment can be carried out on the work itself, including creating areas of light and dark in the process of distressing.

Chemical Stains

The above stains may legitimately be referred to as dyes (and are often sold as such), while true staining (i.e. actually changing the colour of the wood by chemical change) is achieved by a number of chemicals which, when applied to the surface, react with certain substances in the wood itself, creating other coloured chemicals. Not all woods will respond, and even those that do may not stain evenly, because the action depends very much on the concentration of chemicals (notably tannic acid) present in the wood. The colour of the chemical stain bears no relation to the final colour achieved.

The most commonly used chemicals and their actions are:

Bichromate of potash This is orange in colour; a solution of 2oz (56.7g) in a pint of warm water will turn true mahogany a red/brown and oak a warm, mellow brown.

Iron salts In weak solutions these give a silvery tone to oak, and may also be used to kill the redness of mahogany if you want to stain it to resemble walnut. They produce a greyish tone on sycamore to create 'harewood' (especially useful in marquetry and the like). If used in too strong a mixture, iron salts will turn oak inky black. By steeping iron nails in white vinegar overnight and decanting off the liquid, you will have a stock solution of iron acetate. The black discolouration around iron nails and screws in external oak timbers is the result of iron stains.

Ammonia The strongest solution available is called 'point eight eighty' (0.880), and is 35% ammonia. (Household ammonia is between 5% and 15% concentration.) On its own, the 35% solution creates only a slight darkening of oak, but if oak is exposed to the ammonia fumes, the effect is dramatic: the oak progressively darkens and eventually turns grey-black. The process can be stopped at any point by ending the exposure. The resulting oak looks really old, and ammonia can be used when restoring old oak artefacts and structural timbers by placing the article in a 'tent' made of clear polythene sheet, with several saucers of ammonia distributed evenly inside before sealing. The tent allows you to see the change. Small objects can be fumed in inverted fish tanks.

The effect of fuming can be intensified by first swabbing the wood with tannic acid solution – or very strong tea!

Other strong alkalis Caustic soda, washing soda and other strong alkalis will darken oak, mahogany and other hardwoods, which is one reason for not using caustic stripping on these timbers. 1oz to a pint of clean water (28.35g to 0.56l) is a good stock solution, which can be strengthened or diluted as necessary.

There are a number of other chemicals that will stain wood, but the ones listed are those readily available. They can all be obtained from a pharmacist, possibly by special order only, within a day or so.

NGR stains Non-grain-raising (NGR) stains are based on highly volatile solvents. This makes them ideal for production work where the speed of drying is an essential part of the process. They are designed to be sprayed on to the work as a full, wet coat, which may be evened out by hard rubbing with a cloth if required. Any attempt to apply these stains with a brush is likely to result in considerable frustration, with tide marks forming as the solvent evaporates quicker than you can maintain a 'live' edge. There is also the issue of safety hazards. Should you wish, or need, to work with these materials, refer to Chapters 3 and 9.

HEALTH AND SAFETY

As a general rule, all stains should be considered as toxic materials and treated as such, i.e. stored in properly labelled containers and locked away from children and animals.

They should also be considered as irritants, so wear protective clothing and rubber gloves, as many stains can lead to contact dermatitis. Wear goggles when mixing and using ammonia and caustic soda; add the caustic granules gradually to cold water in a bucket, stirring all the time. A great deal of heat is generated, so wait for the solution to cool down before using.

While using ammonia, wear a respirator fitted with a gas cartridge; the fumes are very over-powering and can cause damage to your lungs, especially if you are asthmatic or bronchitic. *See* Chapter 3.

Chemical stains should be applied by pad rather than brush, to prevent any surplus liquid running all over the place. Strong alkalis will also dissolve bristles.

APPLYING STAINS

There are basically two methods: brush and pad.

Brush Decant the stain into a wide-necked container. Use paintbrushes reserved for the sole purpose of staining; charge the brush, and squeeze out surplus from the bristle tips by pressing against the side of the container. On large flat areas such as table tops, apply the stain in straight strokes along the grain, working from the edge furthest away from you and gradually moving towards you. Overlap the strokes slightly as shown in Fig 5.1, so that only one 'live' edge is kept open (this prevents tide marks), recharging the brush as needed. When the whole surface has been covered, take a clean, lint-free rag, dip it into the stain and thoroughly wring it out. Form the rag into a pad and wipe over the work along the grain in straight strokes, to even out the colour. Allow to dry.

When using water- or spirit-based stains, the work can be recoated to darken the shade once the first coat has dried.

The work should be broken down into manageable sections. Do not try to stain a large piece all at once, as the stain will dry before you can even it out. On a table, for example, treat the top as one section, the legs as another, and so on.

Carving and intricate mouldings may need a stabbing action with the brush to ensure that no spots are missed. If this does occur, any areas missed can be touched in with a pencil brush.

Pad This method can really only be used satis-factorily on flat surfaces, mouldings and carvings still needing a brush. Fold some upholstery

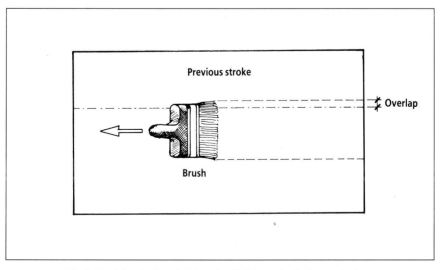

Fig 5.1 Staining by brush. Note the slight overlap between strokes.

Previous stroke

Overlap

Brush

Fig 5.2 A pad used for applying stain.

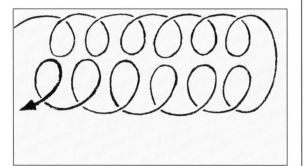

Fig 5.3 The circular path when applying stain by pad.

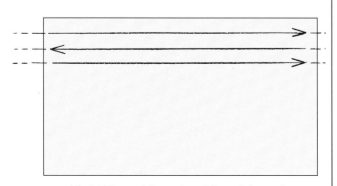

Fig 5.4 The straight strokes of the staining pad.

wadding into a ball, wrap it in a clean, lint-free cotton rag and flatten the face to form the pad, as shown in Fig 5.2.

Dip the pad into the stain and allow it to draw up into the wadding. Squeeze the pad against the side to remove the surplus, and then work the stain over the surface in a circular motion, as shown in Fig 5.3. Apply little or no pressure at first, as the stain will flow freely on to the work, and gradually increase pressure as it dries out. Recharge the pad if necessary. Finish off by working along the grain as in Fig 5.4, to eliminate the circular paths and to even out the colour.

STAINING PANELLED WORK

Fig 5.5 shows the problem of panelling, with stiles, rails, muntins, panels and mouldings. The numbers indicate the order of staining and how the work should be sectioned off. You will need to use a brush and to watch out for runs.

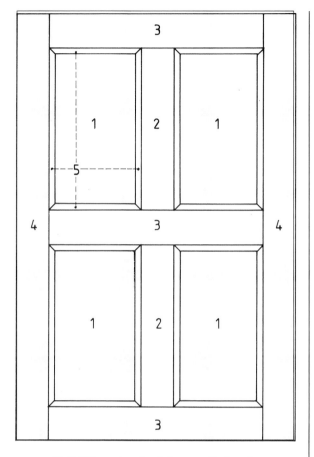

Fig 5.5 The order of staining panelled work.

1 – panels   2 – muntins   3 – rails

4 – stiles   5 – mouldings

BLEACHING WOOD

There will be situations where you will need to eliminate stain marks and the like before dyeing the wood; or you may want to remove as much colour from the wood as possible. Both cases involve bleaching. In the first instance we want to remove the unsightly stain without creating a very obvious light patch, while in the second we need a strong bleaching action. Each case is an example of chemical action on the wood. The two most suitable bleaches are oxalic acid and a two-part wood bleach respectively.

Oxalic Acid

This is a toxic organic acid that a pharmacist will be able to get for you. Wear gloves while using it, and store it safely in well-labelled containers.

Make up a solution of approximately 2oz in a pint of warm water (56.7g in 0.56l), sponge over the whole of the offending surface (which, of course, has been stripped of any kind of finish) and allow to dry thoroughly. Once dry, you may find a whitish deposit on the surface; this is crystals of oxalic acid, which can be brushed off (wearing a mask to avoid inhaling the crystals). Residual acid in the wood has to be neutralised with a solution of 1oz borax in a pint of warm water (28.35g in 0.56l), sponged on and allowed to dry. Afterwards, the surface will be a little fuzzy, due to raised grain, so give a very light sand before staining and finishing. Fig 5.6 shows before and after photographs, showing the effect of oxalic acid on a black ink stain.

Two-part Wood Bleach

Oxygen is, chemically speaking, an extremely active substance. When produced during a chemical reaction, it is so chemically active that it readily attacks organic materials and metals. This introduction to the chemistry of these bleaches is important to remember, as it will determine the safe approach to the use of what are highly dangerous substances. The chemicals in the wood that produce its colour are highly sensitive, and by producing oxygen gas within the wood by chemical reaction, they are attacked and changed to near-colourless materials. This is termed an oxidation reaction.

As their name implies, two-part bleaches comprise two chemicals. One is a strong solution of hydrogen peroxide (typically 100 vol.), and the other is a strong alkali (either 2% caustic soda or 0.880 ammonia solution). You can buy these chemicals individually from a pharmacist (but they normally only sell 20 or 40 vol. peroxide solution), but it is probably better to buy a specially formulated proprietary wood bleach.

Different brands will vary in their instructions for use, but the following outlines the process in principle:

1 Brush the first solution over the wood, taking care not to flood it, and leave for about five minutes. This is the strong alkali, and on some hardwoods you may be horrified to see the wood darken considerably – don't panic, this is quite normal.

2 Brush the second solution over the wood and leave to dry. This is the hydrogen peroxide, and you may witness frothing after a few minutes. Again, this is quite normal, as it is simply the oxygen being released from the peroxide – it may even sizzle.

3 Leave for two or three days to thoroughly dry out. The wood will be furry due to raised grain, and there may be the odd watermark. Gently wash down with a weak solution of white vinegar, and leave to dry for another day or so. Gently sand smooth with a 320 grit paper, not too deeply, as bleaching does not penetrate very far. If the work is not light enough, repeat the process.

There are a few points to remember. The alkali acts as a catalyst, releasing the oxygen from the peroxide which, after drying, is harmless; however, the alkali still remains in the wood, and the vinegar is used to neutralize it.

Secondly, both chemicals are dangerous while in use, and will cause painful skin burns. Wear protective clothing, rubber gloves and eye

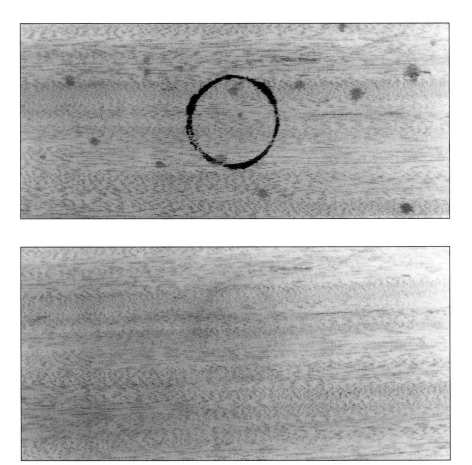

Fig 5.6 Bleaching an ink stain: (a) before, (b) after.

protectors. Hydrogen peroxide may appear to be fairly inoffensive, but it is an oxidizing agent and will release highly reactive oxygen as soon as it comes into contact with metals or organic material. As this will include your skin, any contact with the liquid will result in a chemical burn, the severity of which will be determined by the strength of the peroxide solution.

Use synthetic 'bristle' brushes, as the solutions will dissolve real bristle! Also use separate brushes for each solution, to avoid contamination. Decant each solution into separate and labelled plastic, glass or ceramic containers, and discard unused solutions, as they may be contaminated. If you pour them back into their respective containers, chemical reactions may take place that may cause them to explode. Never use metal containers, as both solutions will react with the metal – the peroxide, in particular, will undergo premature chemical breakdown.

PIGMENTS

Pigments are coloured powders that do not dissolve in a liquid; in this respect they are fundamentally different to stains. When stirred into a liquid, the powders remain suspended for a while before settling to the bottom of the container as shown in Fig 5.7. Their role in wood-finishing is limited, but those uses to which they are put cannot be fulfilled by true stains. For example, if raw umber (which is a dirty, greeny grey) is mixed with wax polish used on pine, it helps create an antique effect by collecting in crevices and giving the surface a general powdery look that normally comes with age. Because pigments lie on the surface of wood, they do give a granular effect worth experimenting with. However, it is best to restrict your colours to the so-called earth pigments (described in detail in later chapters).

Fig 5.7 (left) A stain dissolves in the liquid, which is semi-transparent; (right) A pigment will not dissolve, and clouds the liquid. Eventually, the pigment settles out to the bottom of the container. It is important to agitate any pigment-based mixture, to keep it uniformly mixed.

CHAPTER 6

Wax and Oil Polishing

A part from paint, wax and oil are probably the oldest forms of wood finishes, which gives them the assumed credentials to claim their place as being the most 'natural' and aesthetically pleasing. This view is reinforced by the marketing approach adopted by a number of manufacturers: wax and oil represent good craftsmanship, natural beauty and a reaction against the evils of mass production. This was certainly the view of the furniture makers of the Arts and Crafts movement towards the end of the last century; these designer–craftsmen considered that there had been a debasement of craftsmanship, and so they harked back to an earlier age, devoid of machinery but rich in the high values placed on 'honest' hand crafts-manship – the Middle Ages. Their work was characterized by the almost exclusive use of home-grown timbers, and was simply designed and beautifully constructed, using the classic cabinetmaking techniques. The pieces were frequently left unfinished, or were oiled or waxed.

This is still the image of waxing and oiling, but the same charge can be levelled against them as was made against the indiscriminate use of French polish towards the end of the nineteenth century and the beginning of the twentieth: wax and oil polishes are just as capable of indiscriminate and inappropriate application. 'Rustic' timbers such as oak look well under the low lustre of oil and wax, which leave the surface with a texture and tactile quality that is so admired, but many of the highly figured and richly coloured woods need to be brought alive by the optical properties of 'hard' finishes such as French polish or cellulose lacquer. On a more practical note, the tough mechanical properties of a catalysed lacquer may be more appropriate for the commercial market.

Amongst the most common errors is to attempt to dress varnished, French polished or lacquered furniture with beeswax or furniture oil. All that results from this is a greasy build-up which eventually dulls and masks the surface, as it attracts dust and other pollutants in the air. While some products on the market are specifi-cally designed to be used on these 'hard' finishes, they are of special formulation, and should be used very sparingly and not very often. Bees-wax polish and the various furniture oils such as Danish oil, tung oil and linseed oil, are wood finishes in their own right, and are not designed to be used with anything else.

Before describing the materials involved, Table 3 compares and contrasts the advantages and disadvantages of wax and oil polishes.

TABLE 3

QUALITIES	WAX	OIL
Easy to apply	Yes	Yes
Durability	Low	High
Heat and water resistance	Low	High
Renewability and revival	Yes	Yes

The conclusions from this information are:

▌ As they are easy to apply, a high level of prac-tical skills is not required for these polishes.

▌ Wax polish is vulnerable and therefore not suitable for projects subject to a great deal of wear or exposure to heat and moisture.

▌ Oil is particularly resistant to moisture and hot crockery and can therefore be used on dining tables, coffee tables etc.

▌ Both forms of polish are easily renewed or revived by the application of another coat as they wear.

SURFACE PREPARATION

The procedures described in Chapter 4 should be adopted. If a scraper has been used on oak, polishing can take place without the need for sanding. However, there is a useful technique called burnishing, which helps to give hardwoods an initial sheen by compressing the surface wood fibres.

The burnisher is made from another piece of hardwood, usually beech, which is very hard and close-grained. Its shape is shown in Fig 6.1,

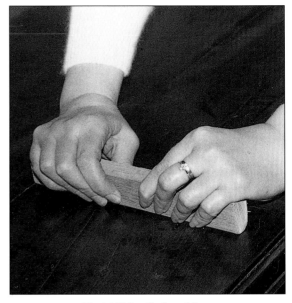

Fig 6.2 Using the burnisher.

and Fig 6.2 shows the burnisher in use. By rubbing the rounded edge of the tool along the grain with as much pressure as you and the furniture can stand, the surface fibres in the furniture are compressed, packing them tightly and creating a sheen. This technique is an old method, and, while not obligatory, it does help to build up the shine quickly. Softwoods such as pine will not burnish too well, and the pressure may cause unwanted indentations. The method is useful when waxing or oiling oak or other home-grown hardwoods such as ash or walnut.

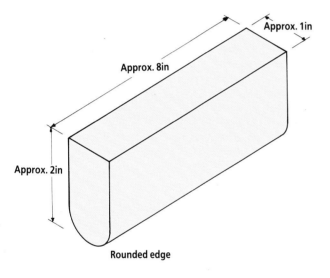

Approx. 1in

Approx. 8in

Approx. 2in

Rounded edge

Fig 6.1 A hardwood burnisher.

WAX POLISHING

Recipes for wax polishes are given in Chapter 16; in essence, they consist of a wax dissolved in a solvent such as turpentine or white spirit. Some formulations rely on a more volatile liquid, akin to petrol, but the fumes they give off are so powerful as to make any extended period of use positively dangerous without using a mask with an effective gas cartridge. Their particular advantage is the speed with which the solvent evaporates, making sure that the polish dries quickly. A wax polish cannot do its job properly until the solvent has all evaporated and only the wax itself remains on the surface. Friction is then used to soften the wax and distribute it as a smooth, thin, lustrous coat, by filling in the pores and lying in a smooth coat over the surface.

Included in the recipes is a formulation for an 'antique' wax. This incorporates a pigment to colour the polish, so that when it is used on bare wood it imparts a colour cast of its own and is supposed to simulate age by giving a very granular look to the surface. This is not an uncommon practice, and can be very effective if used judiciously; apart from giving a general colouring to the surface, some of the pigment tends to become lodged in the corners of mouldings and in corners, suggestive of the build-up of dirt and grime that occurs here in older pieces of furniture or other woodwork.

A number of different waxes may be used, either singly or, more commonly, in combination.

Beeswax

The best known of the polishing waxes, its association with something so obviously natural and within our realm of experience has given rise to a reputation that I am not entirely comfortable with. It has to be said that the pungent odour of turpentine and the sweet, honey smell of the wax is irresistible.

Notwithstanding its very high reputation, this wax does have a drawback or two: there is still only one way to obtain the wax – the time-honoured way – and this makes it expensive, even when you consider the highly commercialized way in which the bees can be reared to produce honey. In use, the wax tends to become a little tacky in warm environments. This may not be immediately apparent in a block of the stuff, but as a thin layer it will fingermark easily, and will also attract dust.

The wax can be bought in blocks, and is white (purified wax) or yellow (natural) in colour.

Carnauba Wax

The outer, shiny skin from the leaves of a Brazilian palm yields this wax. It is very hard and brittle, like homemade toffee, so much so that it is rarely used on its own. A traditionally made beeswax polish can be improved by adding 10% carnauba wax; this has two effects on the properties of the polish. First, it stiffens the polish, making it a little more durable and harder when dry. Second, due to its hardness, carnauba wax produces a deeper sheen than beeswax, so a mixture of the two will have an enhanced lustre.

Paraffin Wax

Candle wax, as it is commonly called, does not have too much to commend itself as a polish, but may be used in cheaper polishes to make the blend less expensive.

Japan Wax

A very expensive blend of vegetable waxes, this has exceptional properties, and is to be found in the best traditionally blended wax polishes.

Synthetic Wax

The best known is silicone wax. Synthetic waxes form the basis of many modern formulations of wax polishes. The silicones in particular have the property of imparting a very high sheen for relatively little effort. The problem, however, is that they create a high build-up and may even trap dust between the layers during each application. Eventually, instead of improving the shine, the surface begins to go dull and patchy.

WAX PASTES AND CREAMS

The stiffer wax pastes are produced by simply dissolving the wax in a suitable solvent (i.e. turpentine or white spirit). The wax content is, in proportionate terms, very high. The pastes need to be applied quite sparingly, to prevent excessive build-up, which makes the finish difficult to buff.

The consistency of the paste can be varied by altering the relative amounts of solvent and wax: the higher the wax content, the stiffer the paste. For the first application or so on to bare wood, the paste ought to be fairly soft, say the consistency of butter on a warm day. It can then be spread more easily and be forced into the pores of the wood, sealing it more effectively. Subsequent applications can be made with a stiff paste, which tends to buff up to a sheen more easily.

Wax creams are rather different: they are formed by emulsifying the wax and solvent mixture in water, and consequently have a much lower wax content, by proportion, than will be found in a wax paste. They are not designed to be used as a finish in their own right, but as a dressing over a hard finish such as French polish, to improve lustre and provide a little measure of additional protection. Because they also contain water and an emulsifying agent, wax creams will have an additional cleaning action on the surface. The consistency of a cream will vary in stiffness from very liquid to being like whipped cream. Creams are mentioned here only to distinguish them from genuine wax polish, as there tends to be considerable confusion surrounding the types and suitability of the different types.

Frankly, there is little merit in making your own polish, as there are so many good proprietary products available. Nevertheless, anyone who has any interest in the subject will usually want to give it a whirl. Recipes and methods of making can be found in Chapter 16.

USING WAX POLISH

I have already stressed the need to be sparing; this is one of those situations where the more you use, the more difficult it becomes to obtain good results. The reason for this is that the sheen is obtained by burnishing the wax to a mirror smoothness. The more wax you put on to the surface at any time, the harder you will need to work to produce the end result. Adopt the rule of thumb: two thin applications are better than one heavy coat.

You will find it useful to seal the surface of softwoods and the more open-grained hardwoods (such as oak or ash) with a coat of transparent French polish. This can be applied sparingly with a brush and then allowed to dry for a couple of hours. By sealing the wood first, you reduce the number of wax applications by at least one coat or possibly two, by building up the sheen much quicker. It also helps to reduce dirt penetration at some later date.

Apply the wax with mutton cloth (stockinette), using a circular motion and forcing it into the grain. Finish off with straight strokes along the grain. Leave the polish to dry for at least an hour, longer if possible, before buffing vigorously along the grain with a new piece of mutton cloth. Alternatively, wrap a piece of terry towelling around a brick and rub along the grain –

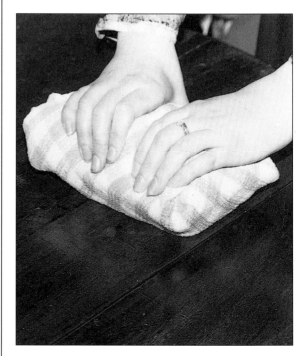

Fig 6.3 Burnishing a waxed surface with an old towel wrapped around a brick.

this is an excellent method for large flat surfaces. *See* Fig 6.3.

Carvings cannot be treated in this way. The polish should be applied with a shoebrush, allowed to dry and then buffed with a clean brush. The main thing to remember is to avoid accumulations of wax in the corners and quirks, as once they dry here, dust and other dirty, unsightly accumulations begin to build up. Finally, buff with a clean cloth.

How many coats of wax should be applied? Waxing produces a better finish with time, as does oiling (*see* page 59). Initially, two or three applications will produce an acceptable surface, but as time goes on and more applications of wax are made over a period of years, the wood surface takes on a warm, mellow glow. It cannot be produced immediately, although hot waxing will go a long way towards it.

HOT WAXING

It has to be said that this technique is not without its attendant risks. The wax is applied hot to the wood, where it will almost immediately cool and solidify. A hair dryer is then used to heat and fuse the hard wax over a small area, and terry towelling is used to rub it well into the wood. Do not seal the wood beforehand.

The method does have a number of benefits, though: the heat aids penetration, and so the wax is driven deep into the surface; this in turn creates a more immediate impression of age, especially if yellow beeswax has been used, than can be created with cold wax, which does not penetrate so deeply. The technique is rather wasteful in that more wax polish is used (a frightening amount really), but the result is worth the additional effort and expense. The obvious situation where its use is recommended is on stripped pine furniture or doors. Once the solvent has evaporated, there remains a pleasant honey odour and a deep, mellow sheen.

Fig 6.4 Double boiler arrangement for melting wax.

Melt the wax polish using a double boiler arrangement, as shown in Fig 6.4. There will be a build-up of solvent fumes, so have plenty of ventilation and wear a respirator mask. Above all, use a very low heat, and preferably an electric ring rather than gas – naked flames are not a good idea from a fire risk point of view. It is best to make your own polish for this; use one of the recipes given in Chapter 16.

Position the work so that the polish is applied to a horizontal surface. Remove the liquefied polish from the heat and apply the liquid to the wood, using a clean paint brush and brushing well out. The wax will begin to solidify as it cools, so work quickly. You will need to recharge the paintbrush regularly. It is not imperative to get entire coverage of the area, as the next stage in the process will ensure this; in fact, it is better to miss some of the area, otherwise there will be too much wax and the towelling will become clogged and useless.

Allow to dry for at least an hour, to ensure that most of the solvent has evaporated. Use the hair dryer to remelt small areas of wax, at the same time rubbing vigorously with terry towelling. As each area is completed, move on to the next until the whole surface has been burnished.

Hot Waxing

1 Fig 6.5 (a) Applying molten wax polish with a paintbrush.

2 Fig 6.5 (b) Melting the dried wax with a hair drier.

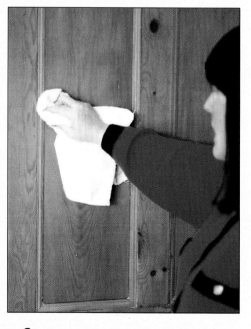

3 Fig 6.5 (c) Rubbing in the liquefied wax with old towelling.

Fig 6.5 shows the entire process. Take care when using the drier. Use the warm setting rather than the hot, and apply only sufficient heat to melt the wax – do not let it linger.

You will find that the towelling will become clogged with wax, and it will be necessary to refold it at regular intervals to present a clean surface. This is important because the process relies on heat and friction, and clogged areas of the cloth will not create the friction.

Maintain the finish with a periodic application of cold wax polish.

OIL POLISHING

Our forebears most commonly used linseed oil as a furniture oil, but they also used other vegetable oils, such as poppy, walnut, olive and hazelnut. These are still the traditional oils, primarily linseed oil, but there are now proprietary products available that offer a number of distinct advantages: they are specially formulated to be particularly easy to apply, become absorbed into the wood faster and dry more quickly. Before looking at the process of oiling, it is worth looking at what benefits oiling has to offer.

The main advantages are that a fully oiled surface (if such a thing actually exists!) is resistant to moisture and heat, making it a suitable finish for dining and coffee tables. Vegetable oils react slowly in the air, harden and effectively form a protective skin. The formulation of proprietary furniture oils includes at least two ingredients apart from oil: a solvent and a drier. The purpose of the drier is to speed up the reaction of the oil with the oxygen in the air – a process called oxidation – which in turn allows a shorter time between applications of oil.

A traditional recipe for a polish based on linseed oil is given in Chapter 16. Note that *raw* linseed oil is specified, and not boiled, which is more viscous and therefore slower to become absorbed by the wood, even though it does dry faster. Proprietary oil blends include teak oil, Danish oil and tung oil, and these offer distinct advantages over linseed oil.

The recipe for this oil polish includes turpentine or white spirit as a solvent whose main purpose is to dilute the oil, to enable it to be more easily absorbed. The first coat is best applied with a clean paintbrush. Don't flood the work, but be generous, without creating puddles. Leave for 24 hours and then rub vigorously with a lint-free cloth to remove surplus oil from the surface. The second coat is applied sparingly with a cloth and left for another 24 hours before rubbing over again. At this stage you may begin to see something of a sheen, but very absorbent wood will need quite a few applications before any real impression is made.

The process of oiling can be made more effective by first warming it, using a double boiler arrangement. The heat makes it more fluid and aids absorption into the surface of the wood.

How many coats and how often? The job of oil polishing is never finished, so it is often said: there is always room for another coat. As a general rule of thumb, for new and stripped surfaces, I follow the regime of one coat a day for a week, followed by one coat a week for a month, followed by one coat a month for a year. By the end of this period, the surface will have gained an unmistakable sheen and silky smoothness. After this, oil may be applied as necessary. The test is whether water runs off without penetration!

Sometimes heat or moisture will cause dulling, but this can be remedied with – yes – another coat or two of oil.

CHAPTER 7

French Polishing

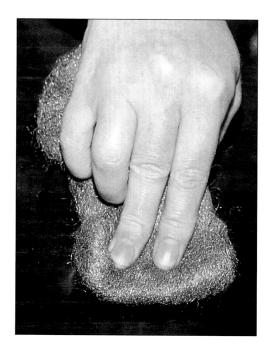

Acres of printed matter have been published on this method of finishing, yet it still retains a mystique and status that is rather baffling. To use modern marketing terminology, it is the most hyped of the traditional finishes, and even today, with all the sophistication of modern finishing materials and methods, the skill of the hand polisher is highly prized and admired.

To a large degree this can be put down to history: French polishing was introduced into this country during the first quarter of the nineteenth century, and the practitioners of the craft immediately kept the process a closely guarded secret. Even today, older craftsmen often refuse to allow others to watch what they are doing.

In truth, the mechanics of the process are straightforward, but its application is notoriously difficult. At best, any written description can only convey the mechanics, although the odd tip here and there concerning working problems and the like will be useful. It is only through practising the technique yourself that the skill can be acquired. Expect disappointing results at first, because there are so many variables that contribute towards a perfect finish that your first attempts will cause you a great deal of frustration. The effort is worth it once the skill is mastered; remember, though, that a good craftsman will never stop learning something new about his or her craft.

An important skill in French polishing is restraint in use. The temptation is to use it everywhere and to create the mirror gloss associated with pianos. A good French polisher is subtle, both with the polish itself and the use of colour. French polish has some serious drawbacks: it will not resist heat, water or alcohol, and even exposure to a damp, cold atmosphere over a period of time (i.e. during storage of furniture) may result in blooming. On the other hand, its smoothness, unique lustre and optical effects on colour and figure make it the most attractive of the hard finishes.

WHAT IS FRENCH POLISH?

French polish is a solution of shellac in alcohol. The concentration of the solution is called the cut, and for general French polishing a three- or four-pound cut is used. This means that three or four pounds (1.35kg–1.8kg) of shellac are dissolved in a gallon (4.5l) of alcohol.

Shellac is a natural product exuded by a certain insect found mainly on the Indian subcontinent, so this area is the main source. There are a number of grades of shellac available, according to the degree of processing the shellac undergoes before being made into polish. There is no real virtue in making your own French polish, as proprietary brands are of a consistent quality, but a recipe is given in Chapter 16.

Garnet This is the darkest of the polishes, made from shellac flakes the colour of garnet stone. When dissolved in alcohol, they form a greenish-red/brown polish that is ideal for use over dark or darkly stained woods.

Button The shellac flakes are a muddy brown colour, and the polish is useful when applied over old walnut which has faded to honey-brown. However, it tends to give a rather unattractive colour cast on brown or reddish timbers.

Orange When made up into polish, this shellac produces a fairly bright orange solution. It is of little value as a French polish, although it can be used to produce tinted polish using red aniline spirit dye. This is the shellac you would be given if buying from a pharmacist.

White White is produced by bleaching dark shellac. It creates a creamy-white polish, and is useful as a general sealer and as a base for tinted polish. Used as a straight finish, if a deep body of polish is built up it will create a slightly grey colour cast, owing to the natural wax present in

Making a Fad

1

Fig 7.1 (a) Folding skin wadding to form a fad: note the fine-textured, fibrous covering (the skin), which sandwiches the cotton wool.

2

Fig 7.1 (b) Cut a square of roughly 30cm sides.

3

Fig 7.1 (c) Fold in half.

4

Fig 7.1 (d) Divide and fold over into thirds, creating the basic pad.

5

Fig 7.1 (e) Form the point along the bullnosed edge by folding in the corners.

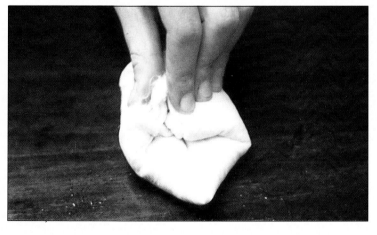

6

Fig 7.1 (f) Form the fad into a pear shape by gripping with your hand.

Making a Rubber

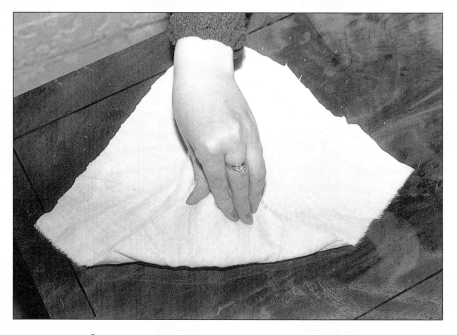

1 Fig 7.2 (a) The point of the fad is aligned with one of
the corners of the rag.

2 Fig 7.2 (b) The corner of the rag is folded over the point
of the fad.

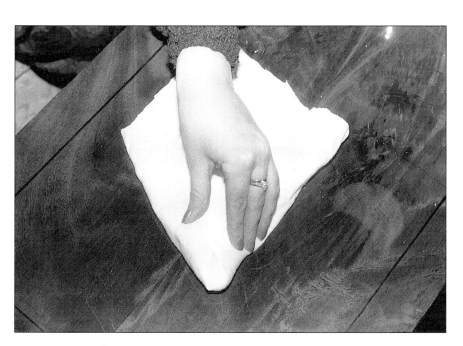

3 Fig 7.2 (c) The 'wings' of the rag are wrapped around
the point to define and maintain it.

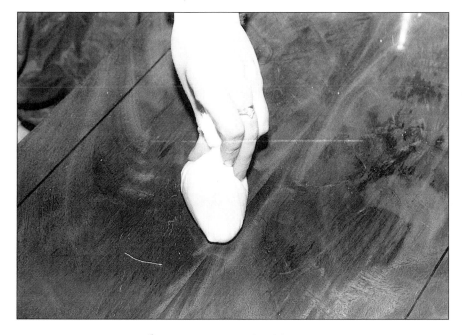

4 Fig 7.2 (d) The 'ends' of the rag are
twisted around.

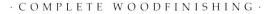

shellac. Because of this, it should be reserved for light-coloured woods, or as a sealer over marquetry, or where the natural colours need to be preserved as much as possible. The flakes have a very short shelf life because of the bleaching process.

Transparent white (or pale) If the wax is removed from white shellac, the resulting polish is a pale amber colour. This tends to be more expensive, because its manufacture is more involved, but it is ideal for use where the colour of the wood is very light or where the colours of inlays and marquetry must be preserved. If a dark polish is used, the natural colours in the wood are modified and much of the benefit derived by contrasting inlays will be lost. There are also transparent versions of garnet and button polish: these retain the colour associated with each, but by taking out the wax, the polish is less muddy and creates a slightly harder finish.

As well as those described above, there are polishes that are described as 'outside' or 'exterior'. These are harder and more resistant to water and alcohol, and can be used on doors subjected to a modest amount of moisture. They are also useful for table tops, if a traditional finish is required. Again, dark and light varieties are available. Table top polishes are shellac-based, but have a formulation which includes ingredients to increase durability. They should not be confused with bar top lacquers, which are a totally different kind of product. Table top French polish has its own thinners, if required.

FADS AND RUBBERS

What distinguishes French polishing from varnishing is the method of application. The French polisher has two very simple, but important, tools for building up the familiar sheen: fads and rubbers. Both are deceptively simple, but their making must be absolutely right. A fad is a pad of upholstery skin wadding, while a rubber is a similar pad over which is stretched a piece of clean, white, fine-grained cotton. How and when they are used will be described later, but it is worth looking at how they are made, as there is a knack to creating perfect fads and rubbers.

Fad

The following description should be read in conjunction with Fig 7.1. A piece of skin wadding approximately 10in (25.4cm) square is cut and laid on a clean surface such as white paper. It is folded in half as shown, and then into thirds. This point, illustrated in Fig 7.1(e), is important and allows the fad to reach into corners. Upholstery wadding is rather springy, and it may be difficult to manipulate the material; if you first soak it in French polish and squeeze out as much as possible, the wadding will behave itself and form the pear shape required without too much difficulty.

Once made, the fad can be left to dry out and harden. Before use it is softened in French polish; this is to 'set' any loose fibres, reducing the risk of them finding their way on to the surface during polishing. In use, the fad is held as shown in Fig 7.3(b).

Rubber

This is the tool that most people associate with French polishing: it consists of a fad made up as described above, which is then wrapped in fine-grained white cotton – old cotton shirts or sheets are ideal. Fig 7.2 shows how the rag, as it is called, is wrapped around the fad. Note that the point of the fad is maintained: this is to allow the fad or rubber to get into corners and angles of mouldings. The method of holding the rubber is extremely important; the bottom needs to be in constant contact with the work, and an even

Holding the Rubber

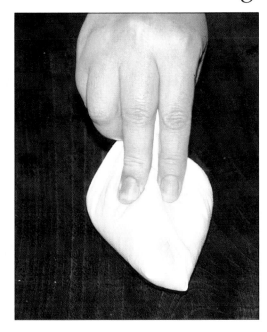

1 Fig 7.3 (a) Holding the rubber too high.

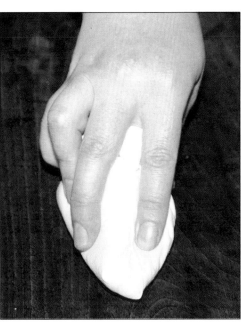

2 Fig 7.3 (b) Correct positioning of the fingers supports the rubber and maintains good contact with the work.

flow of polish through the rag maintained. If held too high up, as in Fig 7.3(a), the rubber will wobble, and you will have little control, resulting in drag marks (rubber burns) and loss of shape. Held as in Fig 7.3(b), the face is pressed against the work, giving you greater control; it will also allow you to feel what is happening, such as the early signs of drag or the tell-tale scraping sensation of grit under the rubber.

Rubbers and fads have to be kept on the move at all times, to prevent them sticking. If for any reason you have to stop in mid-stroke, lift the rubber or fad off the surface without stopping. Bad 'burns' cannot be removed by trying to cover them up – it only makes them worse. Stop, and allow the work to dry for half an hour or so before gently rubbing down and continuing.

Fads and rubbers can be used over and over again if they are stored in airtight plastic or glass containers between periods of use, especially between coats, even though the wait may only be a matter of minutes.

THE WORKING ENVIRONMENT

French polish is very sensitive to the environment during its application and for a period of time afterwards. Keep the temperature at about 20°C (70°F) for the whole polishing period (even between stages, when you are not actually polishing), and for a day or so afterwards while the work is hardening off. If the air is allowed to cool, the polish may bloom as moisture condenses on the surface and becomes trapped in it. The air needs to be free of excessive amounts of dust (no dusty jobs while polishing). In fact, it is a good idea to have a separate room for polishing work, well away from major sources of dust. After cutting back with abrasives – a frequent event in French polishing – make sure that all dust is removed from the surface, using a tack rag. This is imperative to maintain a dust-free environment.

SEQUENCE OF EVENTS

The importance of a meticulous approach to creating an ultra-smooth surface prior to staining cannot be overestimated, as even apparently insignificant blemishes will mar the final effect. Refer to Chapter 4 for the appropriate methods and abrasives, and use shellac beaumontage to fill deep dents and cracks.

Wherever possible, take the work apart and treat each piece as a separate item. For example, take the doors off cupboards, remove drawers and separate the leaves in a table top.

If you want to stain, it is best to avoid using spirit dyes, as the solvent for stain and polish is the same (alcohol), and you run the risk of lifting the colour as you polish. Remember to follow the grain-raising procedure if you water-stain (*see* Chapter 5). After staining, the sequence of events is as follows.

Grainfilling and Oiling

The secret of French polishing is that it is applied as a series of thin layers. Open-textured timbers will draw the polish straight into their fibres; the pores will remain open unless they are filled, and so a mirror finish is difficult to achieve. Filling the grain with a solid material reduces the suction and provides a uniform surface upon which to build the substantial body of polish that is needed. In many instances, though, you may wish to keep an open-grained effect, in which case grainfilling is omitted.

Whether or not the grain is filled, the stained surface is lightly dressed with raw linseed oil.

There are two reasons for this: first, it clears the work of surplus grain filler, and second, it shows up any figure, especially on walnut and decorative veneers.

Fadding

The initial stages of polishing are concerned with satisfying the wood's natural suction and in obtaining a smooth ground on which to apply successive layers of burnished French polish. The polish is applied with a fad.

Colouring

It frequently happens that when you begin polishing, the colour of the work is not right; perhaps it is too red or too green in hue, or the overall colour balance is right, but is too light. It is only after fadding that such discrepancies can be viewed with any degree of certainty and the process of colouring to rectify imbalances be used. (*See* Chapter 5.)

Bodying

Many layers of polish are applied, using a rubber with great care, until the desired depth of body and sheen is acquired. Other books written on the subject refer to the use of raw linseed oil as a lubricant for the face of the rubber to prevent it sticking to the soft, newly applied polish. I have found that this creates more problems than it solves, as the oil has to be taken off again and any residual oil may bleed through later, causing dullness. It also attracts moisture from the atmosphere, increasing the risk of blooming.

If care is exercised, there is no need for oil except on areas which may be creating a few problems. If the rubber appears to want to stick, simply stop and wait for ten minutes or so before continuing. Virtually every student I have taught in the last few years has produced excellent results without the use of oil.

Grain Filling

1 Fig 7.4 (a) Rubbing the plaster into the pores with a circular motion.

2 Fig 7.4 (b) Rubbing excess plaster off the wood, across the grain.

Stiffing (Spiriting)

The last stage in applying polish, this process brings up the surface to a high gloss by burnishing it with the face of a rubber charged with thinned French polish.

Burnishing or Dulling

The high mirror gloss associated with pianos is achieved by burnishing the hardened polish with a very fine abrasive. In restoration work, it is often desirable to reduce the gloss because it looks out of place, especially when compared with original polished areas of the piece. Again, use abrasives to reduce the gloss to an acceptable level.

GRAINFILLING AND OILING

Begin by partially sealing the wood with a brush coat of thinned French polish in a ratio of three parts of polish and one of meths. Apply it quickly and thinly with a polisher's mop; avoid creating runs and ridges, as these are a real problem to eliminate. Allow to dry overnight.

Proprietary brands of grainfiller are available and should be applied according to the manufacturer's instructions, but it is cheaper, and more traditional, to make your own. There are certain situations where grainfiller cannot be used, because it causes problems by lodging in awkward angles, so small mouldings, turnings and carvings are filled with polish; this method will be described later.

Plaster of Paris is the traditional material, with hessian, an open-weave canvas, used to rub it into the pores of the wood. Place a quantity of dry plaster into a wide container, and have ready a separate container of water.

The whiteness of the plaster has to be 'killed' by mixing it with a small amount of powder pigment; the colour of the pigment should correspond to that of the wood (i.e. burnt sienna for reddish surfaces, burnt umber for brownish ones, yellow ochre for golden colours). A stock of different pigments can be built up over a period of time, and should include such colours as burnt and raw umber, and burnt and raw sienna. Mix in enough pigment to take off the extreme whiteness of the plaster.

Pigments can be obtained from a good artists' supplier or one of the trade polish suppliers listed at the end of this book. They are different to stains or dyes in that they do not dissolve in the solvent; this distinction is made clearer in Chapters 5 and 10.

Soak a piece of hessian in water and squeeze it out until it is only damp. Fold it into a pad and dip the face of it into the dry plaster. Transfer the plaster it picks up on to the wood and, working a small area, say 12in (30.5cm) square, rub it into the pores with a circular motion, using a fair amount of pressure. The plaster should form a slurry; before it begins to set, rub off the surplus across the grain (see Fig 7.4). Never allow any surplus to remain, as it will be impossible to remove without damaging the surface once it has set. Pay particular attention to the quirks in mouldings and the angles between adjoining members. Use orange- or matchsticks to remove accumulated filler in these areas, as they will not dig into the wood.

Repeat this process over the whole work to be polished, sectioning it off in small areas. Do not be tempted to cover a large area at once, as the plaster will harden while you are applying it. Allow the filled surfaces to dry and harden overnight. As the work dries, it will suddenly turn white and powdery – this is normal. The pores in the grain will show up as white flecks, with a powdery residue on the surface. There should be no solid build-up.

After overnight drying, the surface must be cleared of the residue and the whiteness in the pores 'killed'. Rub in enough raw linseed oil to restore the original colour; no more, as too much oil will lie on the surface and might bleed through the polish later. Rub off across the grain and leave to dry overnight. Even if the grain has not been filled, oiling is still done, as it enhances the figure. Ensure that all the white flecks have been eliminated by oiling.

FADDING

Give the work a good rub-over with a clean, lint-free cloth to remove residual oil and filler. Make up a fad and charge it with polish in the

Fig 7.5 (a) Charging a fad with polish.

Fig 7.5 (b) Squeezing out the surplus.

following way: pour the polish into a wide container such as an old cereal bowl or cleaned-out margarine tub. Dip the face of the fad into the polish, squeeze out the surplus and distribute the remaining polish throughout the wadding by pressing the face against a piece of clean, white non-absorbent paper (*see* Fig 7.5).

Straight Strokes

Using light pressure at first, apply the polish to the work in straight, slightly overlapping strokes. There should be an obvious full width streak but no ridges, which will be difficult to eliminate later if allowed to dry in. If there are several pieces to be polished, work them in rotation, covering each piece once, then return to the first piece and repeat with a second coat. If only one piece is being polished, wait a few minutes before applying a second and any subsequent coats. After about three coats, a sheen should be starting to appear. Leave the work to dry for about 15 minutes before giving it a very light sand with fine abrasive paper (320 grit), and dust off (*see* Fig 7.6).

Once you have completed this process with all pieces, then the next parts are carried out on each piece in turn, without interruption between each stage. In other words, for the purpose of clarity, the stages have been described as separate entities, although in reality they follow on from each other without a break.

Small Figures of Eight

Change the pattern of application to small figures of eight. Cover the centre of the workpiece, leaving a border of a couple of inches, covering this border separately after working the centre. This is to ensure that the edges are fadded, as it is all too easy to miss small areas here (*see* Fig 7.7). If you realize that a small area has been missed, it is best to leave it until the next coat; if you attempt to go over the missed area again at this point, the fad is likely to stick and begin to tear up, leaving parts of itself stuck to the surface.

Large Figures of Eight

Immediately apply a second coat in large figures of eight (*see* Fig 7.8); this is to eliminate the circular tracks left by the fad before they dry in. Provided the fad is not too wet, it should not stick or cause bits of wadding to adhere to the

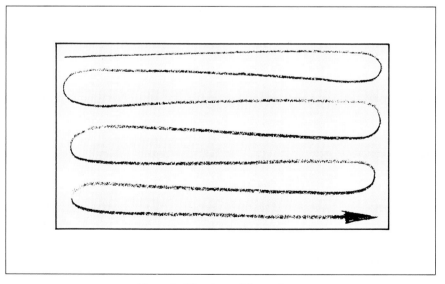

Fig 7.6 Fadding in straight strokes.

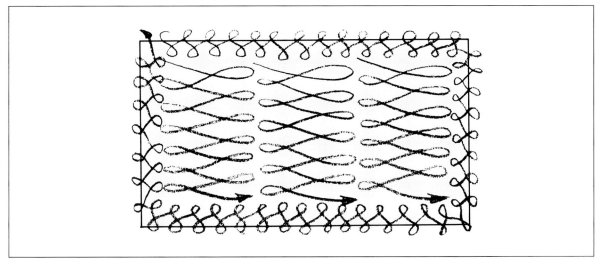

Fig 7.7 Small figures of eight in fadding.

surface; should this happen, stop, pick off the pieces, allow to dry for an hour and gently rub down (320 grit), to remove the odd fibre and flatten the surface before continuing.

Straight Strokes

Finish off by applying straight strokes along the grain. Do not overlap them, as this will be asking for trouble (i.e. sticking). Glide the fad on to one end and off the other (*see* Fig 7.9).

The straight strokes should be just that: avoid arcing the stroke, which would be the natural sweep of the arm movement. For long surfaces, such as a dining table, it may not be possible to complete the stroke in one movement; in such cases, start the stroke at one end and 'glide' the fad off the surface at the midpoint. Cover one half like this and then repeat on the other half. The area in the centre where the strokes meet may show a slight marking, but this will disappear as the polish dries and hardens.

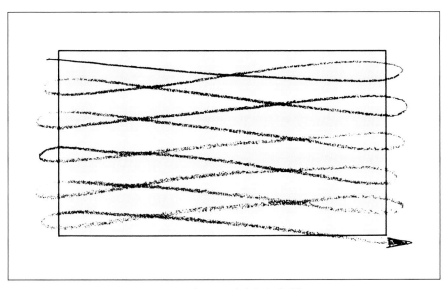

Fig 7.8 Large figures of eight in fadding.

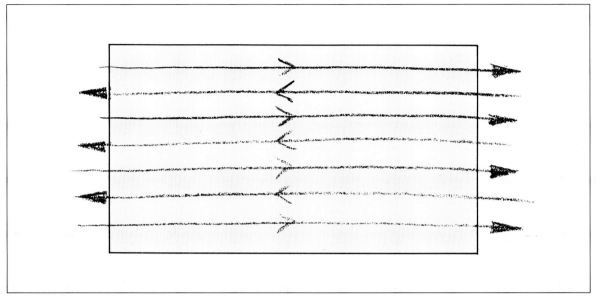

Fig 7.9 Straight strokes.

Allow about 15 minutes for the surfaces to dry before continuing to fad each piece in turn with successive coats, allowing a break of about 10 to 15 minutes between each coat, until there is a definite film over the work. There will be a shine and probably a few dull areas where the fad has dragged, but these do not matter. If the grain has been filled, there should be little evidence of the pores – the surface will be fairly smooth. At this stage the quality of the finish will not be anything to write home about, but that does not matter too much, so long as there are no large pieces of adhering fad, terrible friction marks or ridges.

Allow the polish to harden overnight. After this, you will find that the film of polish has shrunk, and some sinking into the wood will be experienced. Again, this is a normal occurrence, and is one of the main reasons for allowing a long drying period. If polishing is rushed, it may look all right to begin with – a full, mirror gloss – but after a day or so it will shrink back and sink some way into the pores of the wood.

Before continuing, it is now necessary to cut back the fadded film of polish, to create a flawless, smooth ground on which to build a deep, lustrous film. Cut back with a piece of 320 grit abrasive paper, using only sufficient pressure to dislodge adhering particles of dust and fibres of wadding and to create a uniform dullness over the surface, showing no high spots or ridges. Dust off regularly, and use your fingertips to feel the work for any blemishes. Take great care not to cut through the film of shellac to the wood beneath, but if that does happen, restain the bare patch, allow to dry and then apply polish to the area very carefully with a mop. When dry, gently cut back.

It is probably as well to pause here and consider one or two points concerning the use of the fad. The common areas of concern to those learning the craft are: how much polish should there be in the wadding, how much pressure is required, and what happens if the fad begins to stick to the surface?

The fad should be charged with enough polish to create a definite streak on the work, but not so much that the polish pours out and leaves puddles behind it. (The same rule can be applied to the rubber which is used later.) As it dries out, and it becomes difficult to put polish on to the surface, the fad can be recharged.

As for pressure, you should only apply enough to allow the polish to flow on to the surface. The streak of polish should be touch dry very quickly – in seconds rather than minutes. If this is not the case and the film remains wet, then either too much pressure has been used, squeezing out the polish too freely, or the fad was over-charged. During use, the fad will begin to dry out, and it will be necessary to increase the pressure. Recharge the fad when a uniform streak cannot be laid down on to the surface.

The other problem that can occur is that the fad may tend to stick to the surface during a coating cycle. Reduce the pressure on the fad a little if this happens, and things should progress all right. However, the problem can be so bad as to begin breaking up the fad, causing fibres to stick to the polished surface. If this starts to happen, stop; wait half an hour for the surface to dry enough for you to gently remove the fibres with fine abrasive paper before continuing. If you do not feel confident at this stage, you can use a fingertip of raw linseed oil on the face of the fad to lubricate its path – but only a fingertip, and only in the area causing the problem.

Above all, don't forget the golden rule: at all times when the fad is in contact with the work, keep it moving. And if the wadding begins to break up, replace it.

COLOUR CORRECTION

There may be occasions when the colour of the work is not what you imagined it was going to be. A variety of reasons may cause this, and action may need to be taken to correct the error. Chapter 10 goes into some detail of how this correction takes place and of what colour to use, but the general principle involves putting colour into the polish itself and applying it with a rubber, using the same technique as in fadding.

The problems that can arise are an unwanted colour cast (i.e. too much red or green), or the

work being the correct colour, but too light or too dark. Unfortunately, if it is too dark, there is nothing to be done other than strip the work and start again! Most other colour errors can be corrected without stripping. Colour is added to the polish because the wood cannot be stained to effect the correction, as it has been sealed during fadding. The materials needed for this are spirit aniline dyes and insoluble powder pigments.

Once you have applied the corrective layers of coloured polish, allow the work to harden off for a few hours before sealing in the colour with a couple of coats of French polish, applied in straight strokes with a rubber. Allow to dry overnight before proceeding to the bodying stage.

BODYING

If you have stored the fad properly, it should contain enough polish to use as a rubber without recharging. At the same time, it will have been broken in, and its shape established. Convert it to a rubber, as described on page 58.

Test for the quantity of polish by pressing the face of the rubber against a sheet of white paper. Fig 7.10 shows the result of having the right amount, too little or too much. In the last case, open up the wadding and allow it to dry out for a while before retesting and, if necessary, recharging with polish. Fig 7.11 shows how a rubber should be charged: open up the wadding and pour in a small quantity from a bottle. Some workers fit the bottle with a bored bung to control the flow, but if you are careful this is not necessary; anyway, experience will soon teach you how to much to use.

Overcharging will cause ridges that cannot be removed easily, and an excessive flow on to the surface will cause the rubber to stick or 'burn' previous layers of shellac. After charging, press the face of the rubber against white paper as a test and to squeeze out any surplus, distributing

How Much Polish?

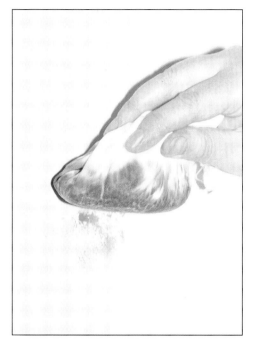

1 Fig 7.10 (a) Too little polish.

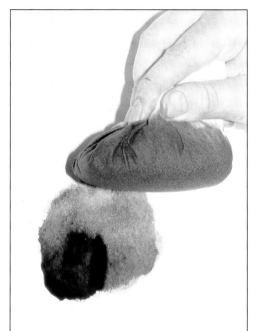

2 Fig 7.10 (b) Too much polish.

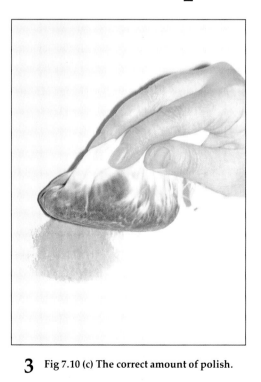

3 Fig 7.10 (c) The correct amount of polish.

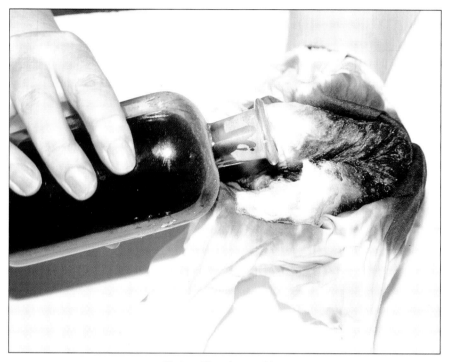

Fig 7.11 Charging a rubber.

the remainder throughout the wadding. Body the work using the following method; again, if several pieces or sections are being polished, follow the sequence for one piece and then each of the others in order, as in fadding.

Figure 7.3(b) illustrates how the rubber is held. Mastering the movement of the rubber is not easy, as the natural way is to use the wrist. In fact, you need to keep the wrist firm and activate the rubber's movement from the elbow and shoulder.

Small Figures of Eight

The centre of the work is bodied with small figures of eight (*see* Fig 7.7). Cover the central portion and then work around the edge, to ensure that the whole piece is covered. The path of the rubber should be obvious, but under no circumstances must there be very wet tidemarks. Stop if the rubber is clearly too wet, and allow the surface to dry for an hour or so before gently cutting back again with 320 grit abrasive.

Large Figures of Eight

Pass straight on to working large overlapping figures of eight along the grain over the whole surface. It may be necessary to divide the surface into two or even three areas if it is very long (*see* Fig 7.12).

By this stage you should be experiencing some resistance to the motion of the rubber. The best way to describe the amount of pull is to carry out a simple experiment: simulate the movement of the rubber by rubbing the ball of your hand over the surface of a clean window-pane. The pull you feel is pretty much like that you need to have during bodying. Apply only enough pressure on the rubber to see the polish being deposited and to achieve the pull just described. Any excessive pressure will cause tearing up, but some friction is needed to pull the polish flat as it is deposited on the surface.

As the rubber begins to dry out, you will need to increase pressure accordingly and then recharge with polish when its face feels warm when tested against the back of your hand. If it feels cold and moist, there will probably be enough polish to continue, but if you are experiencing problems, such as excessive drag or even no drag at all, because very little polish is flowing through, then change the rag, as it is probably clogged. Change the rag if you can see tiny scratch marks or hear the sound of grit under the rubber; you will also be able to detect the presence of grit by the feel of the rubber. Experience will tune your sense of touch to the different responses of the rubber.

Straights

Finally, to eliminate the path marks of the figures of eight, work along the grain with slightly overlapping straight strokes; each stroke should glide on and off the edges. It may be necessary to repeat once or twice if any swirls still remain, in which case take extra care with the pressure you apply, as the risk of sticking is increased. It may be better to recharge the rubber and use light pressure. Experience will again tell you which is better in different circumstances.

When all the pieces to be polished have received a full body as outlined above, allow about 15 minutes or so for it to dry before applying another coat. From now on, the pull on the rubber will increase, so you will need to exercise great care to prevent tearing up the softened polish. There is always the temptation to move the rubber at some speed, but this is a mistake. The rubber movement should always be deliberate, well controlled, and at a slow enough speed to achieve the result without sticking. Any faster, and you will almost certainly tear up the film of polish.

I am frequently asked, 'How many coats?' – a difficult question to answer, as this depends upon a number of factors. Basically, continue bodying until you gain a good, deep sheen or until the rubber is determined to stick to the work. Leave to dry and harden overnight, during which time the film of polish will shrink a little. The following day, if you want a deeper body, cut back with 400 or 600 grit silicon carbide (wet-or-dry) paper, or a piece of very fine nylon pad abrasive, to remove surface blemishes such as rubber marks or adhering dust, before bodying up again. Three or four bodies applied in this way will be enough for some purposes, but for a mirror finish you could need more. You have to judge the situation for yourself.

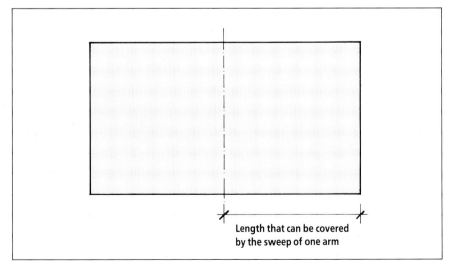

Length that can be covered by the sweep of one arm

Fig 7.12 It may be necessary to divide the work up into two or three sections if the length is too great to cover in one sweep.

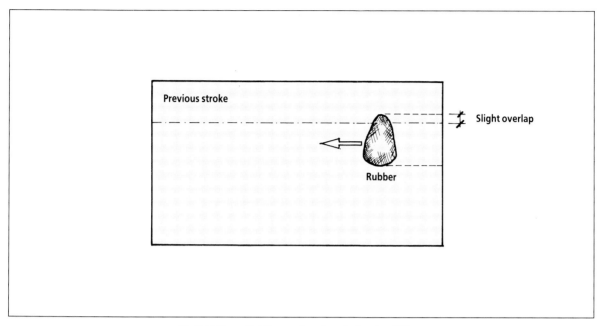

Fig 7.13 Very slightly overlapping strokes in stiffing.

Immediately after each body, there may be minor rubber marks; do not worry about them at this stage, as they should disappear as the polish hardens.

STIFFING OR SPIRITING

In most cases this will be the final stage, which is designed to burnish the polish to a high gloss. Many writers describe the process using pure methylated spirits in a rubber, but this is risky as the powerful solvent action will very likely burn up the polish, ruining all your work. It is much better to use French polish thinned down a little with methylated spirits in a ratio of three parts of polish to one part of meths. Make up a new rubber and reserve it for stiffing only, storing it separately from your bodying rubbers.

After leaving the polished work to harden overnight, cut back the film very slightly with a very fine grit. I find an abrasive impregnated nylon pad in its very fine grade very useful for this job during bodying, as you only have to gently rub away any imperfections, and no more.

Charge the stiffing rubber with the polish and proceed, using very light pressure, as though applying another body, finishing off with straight, very slightly overlapping strokes (as in Fig 7.13). When all the pieces have been treated in this way, wait a few minutes and then repeat. This time you should experience a very definite pull (hence the term stiffing) as the surface film is partially dissolved and pulled flat by the rubber. Two or three coats, with a few minutes between, should be enough. As always, adopt the rule that if you experience difficulty, stop, wait half an hour, and start again.

Finally, allow to harden overnight. There may well be some slight blemishes, such as minor rubber marks: these are not usually a problem, as they disappear as the polish hardens. If not, repeat the stiffing process.

OTHER FINISHING METHODS

For most purposes stiffing produces a really good finish, but there are other ways, each of which is done after stiffing.

Burnishing

This will produce the classic mirror finish often associated with pianos. A very deep body of polish is needed to make it effective, and grain-filler must be used to give a full grain. If you attempt to burnish an open-grained finish, the burnishing cream will collect in the pores and turn them white.

After stiffing, allow the work to harden for at least a day in a warm environment. Special burnishing creams can be bought. Pour a little of the cream on to a damp polishing cloth and quickly distribute it evenly over the whole surface, without applying any pressure. Burnish the surface, using straight strokes along the grain and only a little pressure. As the cream begins to dry, stop and wait for it to dry fully before wiping off along the grain with a soft, dry polishing cloth. It may be necessary to repeat the burnishing process if it has not reached the full mirror gloss. Any residual haze can be removed using a reviver (*see* Chapter 13 for information on how to use a reviver, and Chapter 16 for recipes).

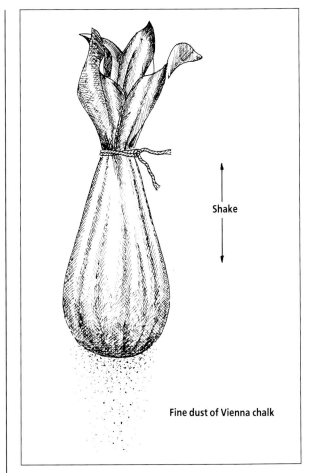

Shake

Fine dust of Vienna chalk

Fig 7.14 The pounce bag.

Fig 7.15 (a) The acid finish: using the pounce bag.

An alternative method of burnishing uses a very fine abrasive called Vienna chalk. The surface is moistened with a cloth soaked in 5% sulphuric acid and then lightly dusted over with the chalk, using a pounce bag made from a square of open-weave cotton (*see* Fig 7.14). A tablespoon of powder is placed in the centre and the corners of the cloth are brought together and tied to form a bag.

Take a clean, damp chamois leather and fold it into a pad. Using very little pressure, rub the leather in straight strokes along the grain until the desired sheen is obtained. Allow the surface to dry before carefully wiping off the chalk dust with a tack rag. Use a reviver to remedy any haze. This is the traditional method of burnishing, called the 'acid finish', and was extensively used by piano polishers (*see* Fig 7.15).

A pharmacist will make up the acid, but to make your own use the following procedure:

5ml of acid is added to 95ml of distilled water in a large plastic container (to prevent splashes). **The acid is always added to the water – never the other way around** – drop by drop, very slowly, as a great deal of heat is generated.

Wear rubber gloves, eye protectors and protective clothing. The solution is ready to use when it has cooled; store it in a properly labelled glass or plastic container.

Dulling

The high gloss left by stiffing may be too much (as may be experienced in restoration work), and must be dulled down. There are two ways in which this can be done (*see* Fig 7.16):

Pumice powder This is lightly dusted over the hardened polish using a pounce bag, and a soft-haired brush is stroked along the grain in slightly overlapping strokes. By gently shaking the bag over the surface, a fine layer of pumice is spread over it. The action of the brush is to create tiny scratches that run along the grain direction and so reduce the gloss. The amount of dulling is controlled by the number of times you brush over the work. When you have finished, under no circumstances wipe off the dust: blow it off, as scratches across the grain will be obvious. Finally, wipe off any remaining particles along the grain with a damp duster, using no pressure.

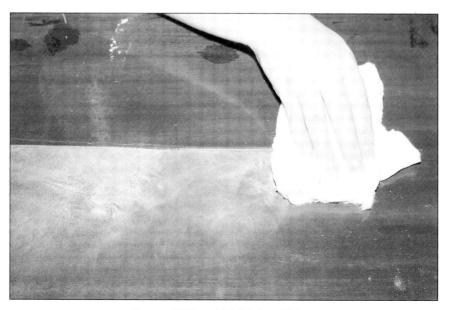

Fig 7.15 (b) The acid finish: burnishing.

Dulling

1 Fig 7.16 (a) Dulling with steel wool and wax polish.

2 Fig 7.16 (b) Dulling with pumice and a soft brush.

The point to remember is that the brush has to be drawn along the direction of the grain, never across it, otherwise the scratches will be distinguishable.

Steel wool and wax This is the easiest and most common way of dulling a gloss finish. Its effect is to reduce the gloss while giving the polish a look of many years of hand buffing. The finest grades of steel wool (000 or 0000) are used. Make up a generous sized pad of wool, dip it into the wax polish and rub the pad over the work in full-length strokes along the grain. Renew the wax if the pad works dry. Again, the amount of dulling is determined by the pressure you apply and the length of time spent rubbing. Allow the wax polish to dry, and buff with a warmed polishing cloth (the heat helps to

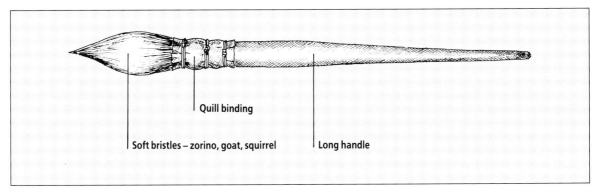

Quill binding

Soft bristles – zorino, goat, squirrel

Long handle

Fig 7.17 Polisher's mop.

distribute the dried wax). A word of warning: do not be too heavy-handed with the wax, or you will have a terrible job trying to remove it during the buffing stage.

POLISHING AWKWARD AREAS

This chapter has so far explained how to polish a straightforward, flat surface. Many items will have areas that are inaccessible to a fad or rubber, such as carvings, intricate or small mouldings, and corners. This is where the polisher's mop and squirrel pencil brushes come in. A mop is a very soft-haired brush, with goat or squirrel hair, or a combination of hair called zorino – this latter being the most useful kind – quill-bound to the handle (*see* Fig 7.17).

Carvings and mouldings Use the mop to apply polish in both fadding and bodying. Stiffing is not possible. Apply thinly, as runs and drips are to be avoided. On carvings, work the polish well into the crevices and undercuts. Mouldings can be burnished or dulled.

Corners Even a well-made fad or rubber cannot reach right into all the angles, which will appear dry. Use a squirrel pencil brush to apply polish into these areas (*see* Fig 7.18).

POLISHING FAULTS

There are several things that can go wrong while French polishing:

Bloom The polish will go dull, and may show a milkiness during application in an environment which is cold and damp, or if a draught is blowing directly over the surface. Cut back after allowing time to harden, adjust the working environment and recommence polishing if the problem is not too great. However, if the surface is badly bloomed, you may have to strip it and start again.

Rubber burns Caused by too much pressure or too wet a rubber; the symptoms are dullness and, in bad cases, a degree of roughness. Allow the work to harden, cut back and polish again.

Fingerprinting If the work is handled too soon after polishing, it may show the impressions of fingers and hands, even though it appears hard. Again, allow to harden, cut back and repolish.

Fig 7.18 Pencil brush used to apply polish in crevices and sharp angles.

Varnishes

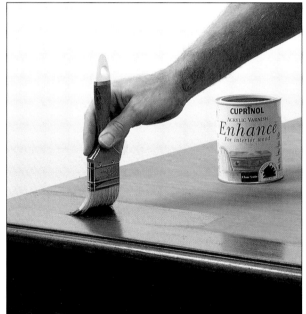

y *Pocket Oxford Dictionary* defines a varnish as 'a resinous solution' – very helpful! In fact, it is a pretty good definition: varnishes are thought of as finishes that are brushed on and allowed to go hard. Not so. French polish is a varnish, and modern spray lacquers are descendants of the early varnishes used 300 years ago. This is because we classify as a varnish any solution of a gum or resin in a solvent which dries to produce a hard and transparent finish.

The early varnishes seem to have derived from the use of oil as a polish. Considerable secrecy surrounded the manufacture and application of these varnishes, but it has been more or less established that many craftsmen were using materials manufactured by dissolving copal resin in linseed oil (and even alcohol in some cases). The basic formulation of varnishes has not fundamentally changed over the centuries in terms of general principles, although the materials have become increasingly sophisticated.

Over the last few decades the chemical industry has provided us with a whole array of new synthetic resins with carefully controlled properties that now give us the ability to choose a finish on a 'horses for courses' basis. In other words, if you want a varnish to do a particular job, then it already exists or it will be invented if the demand for that property makes it commercially viable to do so.

A classic example of this is the development of durable water-based products in response to the desire for a 'safe', solvent-free formulation. The rise of these products has been brought about by increasing market and statutory demands. From a consumer's point of view, they are a dream – easy to apply, minimal odour (therefore no respiratory irritant factor), fast drying and, perhaps the greatest convenience, the ability to clean brushes in water and detergent (no rows of dry, ruined brushes in gummed-up jamjars!).

TYPES OF VARNISH

Polyurethane

Heralded during the 1960s as a significant break-through in paint and varnish technology, this polymer was marketed on the basis of its extreme hardness and durability.

In fact, these very properties are also its source of weakness – brittleness. Polyurethane is not particularly elastic, and if subjected to conditions in which the expansion and contraction of the subject is taking place routinely, then the varnish film will ultimately crack and flake away. It follows from this that polyurethane is much better suited to interior use; while there are specially formulated polyurethane varnishes for use out of doors, they do not have the durability of other products.

Other problem areas are window boards subject to condensation running on to them from the glass, and strong sunlight (or, more specifically, the sun's heat), as the extreme fluctuations in moisture levels within the wood and the expansion and contraction due to the temperature changes will cause rapid breakdown on the varnish film.

Alkyd Resins

This material is the basis of the external varnishes frequently referred to as 'yacht' or 'marine'. They are heavy-bodied varnishes and require longer drying periods than polyurethane. If brushed on too thickly, they easily 'sag' (wrinkle), and take forever to dry. They are less brittle than polyurethanes, and so will move with the wood to some degree. They are also more resistant to corrosive chemical attack, hence their use in marine environments.

Ultraviolet absorbing pigments are used to manufacture coloured varnishes. Sunlight is destructive, not only because of its heat but also because of the chemical activity of UV on organic materials, which deteriorate through long-term exposure. These pigments help to protect the wood by blocking the rays.

Acrylic Resins

The current preoccupation with developing solvent-free products has yielded these water-based varnishes, which are a welcome addition to the marketplace. One manufacturer markets a specially formulated acrylic/polyurethane blend for use on floors.

Since water-based products dry very quickly, compared with traditional varnish drying times, the convenience factor alone makes them a good investment. If a varnish can claim to be recoatable within two hours, it is possible to complete a three-coat varnishing job within a single day!

The varnish also looks different in the can. Open a tin of clear polyurethane varnish, for example, and peer into a transparent, pale amber liquid. Open a can of acrylic, and you are presented with a thick, opaque, milky-white liquid; this can be somewhat alarming if you are not expecting it, but it does dry clear. The appearance is due to the fact that the resins used in the varnish are not soluble in water, and so have to be emulsified.

Microporous

Technically speaking, these varnishes are de-scribed as 'moisture vapour permeable' (MVP). Their claim to superiority over all the other varnishes on the market is their ability to tolerate what, to others, is normally an unacceptable level of moisture in the wood (providing it is not actually wet). Moisture trapped in wood will gradually evaporate and try to escape; all other types of varnish will eventually crack and peel as a result of this, but MVPs actually allow the vapour to escape through the varnish film

(provided it is not too thick), but at the same time provide a barrier against rain, etc. In effect, the varnish allows the wood to 'breathe' by providing what you could describe as micro-scopic pores (*see* Fig 8.1). If at the same time you combine this property with preservatives and ultra-violet filtering pigments, you have the basis of an extremely useful exterior grade varnish. MVP products, if properly applied, will generally last longer than alkyd varnishes. It is pointless putting an MVP over an existing non-MVP varnish (even if it is sound), because the original coat will obviously not allow vapour to pass through. If you intend to use an MVP, you must strip off all traces of any other finish.

Most MVPs are solvent-based, but the latest generation of exterior varnishes is water-based. Other situations in which they may be used are the high humidity environments of kitchens and bathrooms.

COLOURS AND FINISHES

Varnishes can be obtained clear (uncoloured), pigmented (stain varnishes), matt, satin (egg-shell) or gloss. It is beyond the scope of this book to describe individual products, as there are so many and the choice available can cause confusion in the prospective customer, who may or may not have adequate experience of their use. Names and addresses of varnish manufacturers, who are willing to send explan-atory information, are given at the end of the book.

Varnish stains have several advantages over using a stain followed by a clear varnish: first, you are saving time; second, because they are heavy-bodied, they do not become absorbed too deeply into the wood. This makes them ideal for wood of a variable absorbency, which would lead to patchy staining. Varnish stains will produce a more even colour. The main problem with them, however, is that they cloud the surface, especi-

MVP Varnish

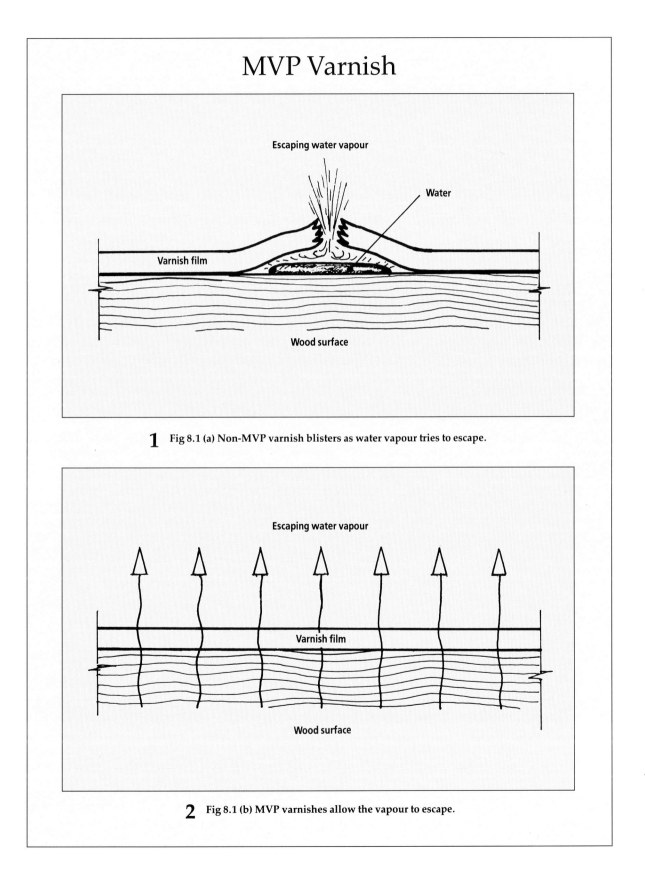

1 Fig 8.1 (a) Non-MVP varnish blisters as water vapour tries to escape.

2 Fig 8.1 (b) MVP varnishes allow the vapour to escape.

PHOTOGRAPH COURTESY OF HAMILTON ACORN LTD.

Fig 8.2 A Hamilton's Namel-Var varnish brush.

ally the darker colours. The figure in the wood becomes obscured if you put more than one coat on, because of the pigments. You can compromise by using one coat of pigmented varnish followed by clear top coats.

The choice of finish is one of personal preference, but many internal surfaces look better with a satin, rather than a full, gloss. This is particularly the case with large areas such as panelling. The reflective surface of gloss may well diminish the effect of the wood's figure, and can result in an unattractive, treacly finish unless meticulous attention is paid to surface preparation and varnish application. This is a matter of opinion, but it does highlight what was said in Chapter 1 about planning and asking yourself some very pertinent questions.

VARNISH 'SYSTEMS'

Several manufacturers produce 'systems', i.e. two or more coating materials designed to be used in conjunction with each other. They are designed for exterior use, and meet stringent architects' specifications, for which they were really developed. They incorporate a means of preserving the wood as well as colouring and varnishing. They usually comprise a coloured first coat preservative, followed by top coats of coloured protective varnishes (usually referred to as woodstains). The first preserving coat will protect the wood for a given period, and so can be factory applied, making the wood safe until final finishing can take place. For this reason it is a very commonly used system in the building trade. All the major paint and varnish manufacturers produce their own products of this type.

VARNISH BRUSHES

It is important that you reserve a special set of brushes for varnishing alone. On no account should those already used for paint be used, as the varnish will be contaminated with specks of paint. As in most things, the best results are more easily obtained by using the best tools. Traditional varnish brushes are oval in cross section, which allows the bristles to 'flow' around edges and mouldings; Hamiltons produce such a brush under the name 'Namel-Var' (*see* Fig 8.2). They can, of course, be used for paint as well, but in view of their considerable expense

Fig 8.4 Keeper varnish.

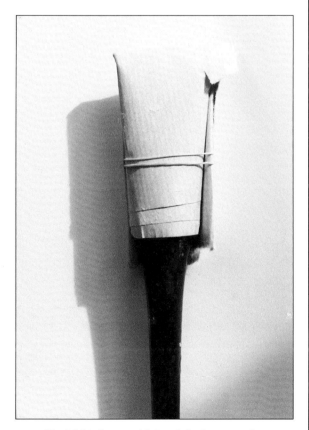

Fig 8.3 Storing varnish brush for future use by protecting bristles.

(but worth every penny) I am certainly not going to do so, and I have made it a capital offence in my family!

Remember, cheap brushes always drop their bristles in the varnish film.

If you have spent a lot of money on a brush, you will want to keep it in good condition. When you have finished varnishing, clean it several times in white spirit and finally in a proprietary brush cleaner, rinsing it out in cold water. Warm water is all that is needed for a water-based varnish. If you are not intending to use the brush in the near future, wrap the bristles in brown paper as shown in Fig 8.3, and store it in such a way that the bristles do not become bent.

The brush should not be cleaned between coats, as the bristles become more pliable and softer with use, producing a better finish. If this pliability can be maintained between coats, varnishing is actually pleasurable. The bristles must be kept wet with varnish, and you will need a glass container and keeper varnish. (Most people have put the brush in a jar of turps, only to suffer the effects of runs when it is used for the next coat!) Keeper varnish is thinned varnish in which the bristles of the brush are suspended without touching the bottom of the jar, so they do not become bent. Fig 8.4 shows a keeper jar; note the cover which prevents dust settling and the nail through a hole in the handle to keep the bristles clear of the bottom. The varnish is thinned in the ratio of three parts varnish to one part of white spirit. A clean, lint-free rag is used to remove surplus varnish prior to recoating.

SURFACE PREPARATION

The work is prepared in the usual way, paying particular attention to eliminating dust with a tack rag. Solvent-based varnishes are generally slow-drying, and will readily pick up dust. Initial cleanliness at the preparation stage will help to reduce the final number of dust specks that will need to be removed for a fine surface.

Previously varnished surfaces that are sound, i.e. not peeling, may be recoated without stripping, but must first be washed down with water and mild detergent, allowed to dry and then 'keyed' by being rubbed down with fine abrasive paper. If the finish is peeling, it will have to be stripped; and if you intend to use an MVP varnish and the old finish is not MVP, then it must be stripped, even if it is sound.

There are one or two points to remember: if the work is being stained, water stains will provide no problems of compatibility, but there may be a problem with oil stains. These are based on the same solvent as most varnishes (except acrylic), and there is the risk of lifting the stain when brushing on the first, thinned coat of varnish. This can result in patchiness, especially if you have not allowed a long drying period for the stain. It is a good idea to apply a thin brush coat of transparent French polish as an isolating barrier. Unfortunately, you cannot do this with MVP varnishes or with exterior work, as the shellac will not allow vapour to escape. If you allow plenty of drying time for the stain and do not become too vigorous in brushing on the first coat, it should not create the problem – but remember that the risk is there.

Acrylic varnishes are compatible with all types of stains.

It goes without saying that you will be wasting your time if the wood is wet, even with MVPs. Allow the wood to dry out for some time before any finishing.

APPLYING THE VARNISH

Whatever type of varnish you are using, the basic rules are all the same: absolute cleanliness of tools and surfaces, a strict adherence to drying times recommended by the manufacturer, and several thin coats rather than one thick.

New, Previously Unfinished or Stripped Surfaces

These will be rather absorbent, so thin the first coat with 10% white spirit (water in the case of acrylics) by volume. Apply fairly generously, avoiding runs. Remove any bristles that find their way on to the work as soon as you notice them, and never allow them to dry in.

When thoroughly dry, 'denib' (remove dust specks) with 240 grit abrasive paper, taking care not to cut through to the wood, and tack rag the surface clean of dust. Subsequent coats should be applied unthinned and each cut back with 600 grit wet-or-dry, using water and a little washing-up liquid as a lubricant. Dry and then tack rag before applying the next coat. The final coat is not cut back unless you are burnishing or dulling (*see* below).

Brushing on Varnish

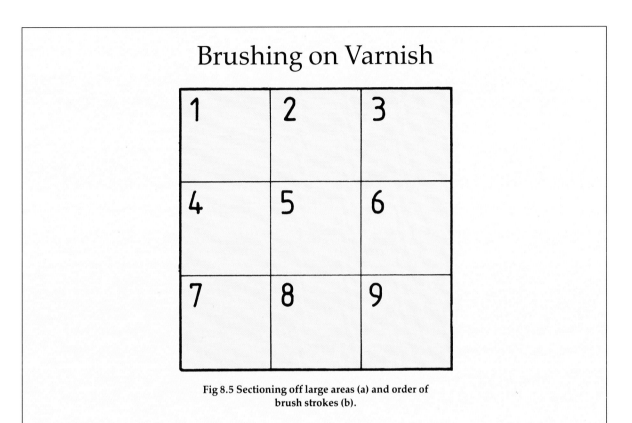

Fig 8.5 Sectioning off large areas (a) and order of brush strokes (b).

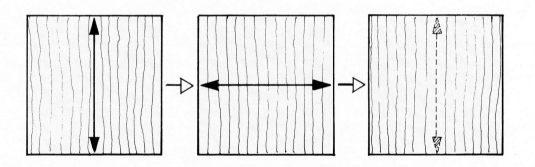

Grain direction

Finishing strokes along the grain

The number of coats depends upon the circumstances: in general, the more wear or the more adverse the conditions are, the more coats will be needed. The exception to this is MVP varnish, where no more than three are applied, or the microporosity becomes diminished. Furniture should receive two or three coats, floors at least four (more in heavy traffic areas); four coats of yacht varnish should be used on external woodwork. If you intend to burnish the varnish to a high gloss, apply one extra coat (not applicable to MVP).

Old, Sound Varnished Surfaces

Wash these down with water and a little washing-up liquid, and allow to dry. Provide a key by rubbing down well with 240 grit paper, and tack rag clean of dust. The work is now ready to receive two coats of varnish (one if MVP), with the wet or dry treatment between them.

BRUSHING TECHNIQUE

How you use the brush goes a long way towards producing a good finish. Narrow sectioned timber such as legs and rails, has the varnish brushed on along the grain, while larger areas, such as table tops, panels and floors, require a different technique to ensure every portion is covered. The brush is charged with varnish to two-thirds of the bristle length, and the tips squeezed against the side of the container. Large areas are varnished in sections, each the size capable of being covered by, say, two or three

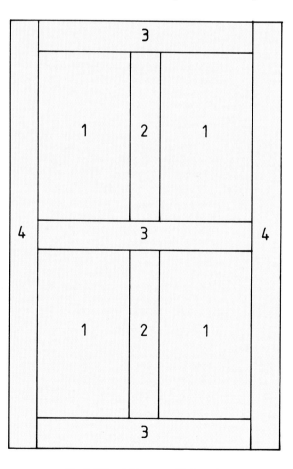

Fig 8.6 Varnishing panelled work.

brush loads. The varnish is first brushed out along the grain, then across it. Finally, the bristle tips are drawn very lightly along the grain in straight strokes to eliminate any brushstrokes. Move on to the next section, and repeat until all the surface is covered. Each section should overlap very slightly so that there are no 'dry' areas. Fig 8.5 illustrates this approach. Fig 8.6 shows the order of varnishing panelled work. The arrows show the direction of the finishing strokes, which correspond to the grain direction.

ALTERNATIVE FINISHES

Varnished surfaces can be burnished to a mirror gloss or dulled to semi- or full matt, though it is easier to use satin or matt varnishes for this. In all cases the varnish should be allowed to harden for as long as possible; at least 48 hours for polyurethane, and up to a week for yacht varnish.

Burnishing

The surface must be free of all blemishes such as dust specks and brush marks, and must be perfectly flat. To prepare for burnishing, the varnish film needs to be cut back with 600 grit wet-or-dry with water and detergent, until all blemishes are removed and there are no bright, glossy areas. Wipe, allow to dry and then tack rag. Special burnishing creams can be bought, but 'T-Cut' or a similar abrasive fluid – even metal polish – will do.

Slightly dampen a pad of mutton cloth large enough to fit into the palm of your hand, and spread enough cream over its face to cover the work. Distribute the burnishing cream over the surface without any pressure, then apply pressure in circular motions over the whole surface until the shine returns, remembering not to linger in any one area too much. Finally apply pressure along the grain. Clean off the cream with a clean cloth, allow to dry and then buff

along the grain. A haze may remain, but this can be removed with a reviver (*see* Chapter 16).

A surface in which the pores of the wood can be seen should not be burnished, as the cream will accumulate in the small cavities, leaving an unsightly white deposit which is difficult to remove. If necessary, apply more coats of varnish to achieve full grain condition.

Dulling

A gloss varnish can be dulled down to a full matt by gently rubbing along the grain with 0000 wire wool; the very tiny scratches destroy the gloss. On the other hand, you may still want a sheen, but may dislike the 'plastic' high gloss that a varnish can sometimes give. In this case lubricate the wire wool with some furniture wax – not too much, otherwise you will end up with a greasy surface – and then buff when the wax has dried, after an hour or so. You can vary the degree of dulling by using different grades of wire wool: 0000 wool with a light pressure will produce an almost burnished sheen, while 0 will produce a significant dulling.

THE VARNISHING ENVIRONMENT

It is not always possible to operate in ideal conditions, especially with exterior work, and you can expect to have to compromise to some extent. The best conditions for varnishing are:

▌ A warm dry atmosphere to aid drying, avoiding direct sunlight. For exterior work, this limits the times to spring and summer. Begin and finish work as early as possible, to allow maximum drying time before the chill of the night arrives (which also increases damp).

▌ A dust-free atmosphere! Although this is impossible, reduce any disturbance of already settled dust: this means not moving anything (if at all possible), and certainly means no woodwork in the workshop at the same time as varnishing. Constant use of the tack rag before varnishing surfaces is important – you can't always see the dust until the varnish is applied. If there is a dust-lifting breeze, don't varnish.

VARNISHING FAULTS

Most varnishing problems arise because of poor environmental conditions, inadequate preparation or careless application. The commonly occurring faults are:

Nibs

These are adhering particles which have become trapped in the varnish film. To a degree they are unavoidable because of the extended drying times of solvent-based varnishes – but they can be reduced. Adequate sanding between coats prevents the cumulative effect of new particles being added to the previous crop; this and careful dusting down with a tack rag are essential practices. The working environment may be difficult to control, but be sensible. Nibs are most disfiguring on gloss finishes, as they are very obvious. The burnishing technique described above will overcome this problem.

Tackiness

If a varnish film is still tacky after the recommended drying time, the following may be the causes:

▌ Cold or damp working environments will inhibit the evaporation of solvent from the film. The remaining 'solid' component of the varnish will not harden either.

▌ Heavy coating, especially with heavy-bodied varnishes such as yacht varnish. The problem here is that the film of varnish 'skins' over: the surface dries trapping wet varnish beneath it,

and the solvent can now only escape very slowly, with a resulting extension of drying time. Be particularly careful with yacht varnish: it is better to apply several thin coats rather than one heavy.

▌ Old varnish may have deteriorated to a point where it will not dry properly because certain active ingredients responsible for speeding up the drying may have evaporated off. If you must use an old tin of varnish that has been knocking around in the (cold, damp) garage, then add a dash of paint drier (terebene), just in case.

Bloom

Varnish applied to damp wood or in damp conditions may develop a milky, opalescent surface, caused by moisture trapped in the varnish as the solvent evaporates. In mild cases, a thorough sanding should eliminate the bloom, but in the extreme example of where the film is practically white, there is no alternative to stripping and revarnishing, after the wood has been allowed to dry or environmental conditions improve. I have seen this effect wholesale on cladding that was fixed to a wall affected by condensation, and it is extremely disfiguring. It does not always occur straight away, and may develop some months after the varnish was applied. Whenever it occurs, damp is the culprit. If you suspect this possibility, use a microporous varnish.

Sagging

A fault found mostly on vertical or sloping surfaces, resulting from loss of adhesion between coats of varnish. Runs and drips occur almost immediately the varnish is applied, but sagging may happen long after the varnish has apparently dried. Loss of adhesion will result from one of two causes, often the combined effect of both (see Fig 8.7).

Bad surface preparation will prevent a good bond between coats, especially if there is grease or dirt present. Combine this with an excessively thick coat of varnish applied over it, and you have the perfect combination for sagging. The top coat may 'hold', and even apparently dry, but gravity may have other ideas. The weight of the film may be greater than the adhesive force holding it to the previous coat. The new coat will begin to slide off, and the result is sagging.

VARNISHING FLOORS

The main properties of a varnish designed for finishing floors are extreme durability and rapid drying, allowing recoating within as short a period as possible. This reduces the amount of dust fallout from the air that becomes trapped within the surface – especially important if a high gloss is required.

Most manufacturers produce a floor varnish, which should be used in preference to ordinary varnishes. All floor varnishes are based on relatively fast-drying solvents and polymers. One or two require an extended period when the floor cannot be used, to allow time for the varnish to harden or cure by chemical action. Clearly, these will produce very tough finishes, but may be rather inconvenient. At the other end of the scale, there are water-based (acrylic) floor varnishes that are very fast-drying and allow you to recoat within a couple of hours. In theory, you could finish a varnishing job within the day, making this type ideal for areas that are in constant use.

You may have to compromise to a degree, in that a traffic lane has to be kept open; varnish the rest, and come back to the area left clear once the rest has hardened sufficiently to use. This may produce problems in colour matching if you are staining.

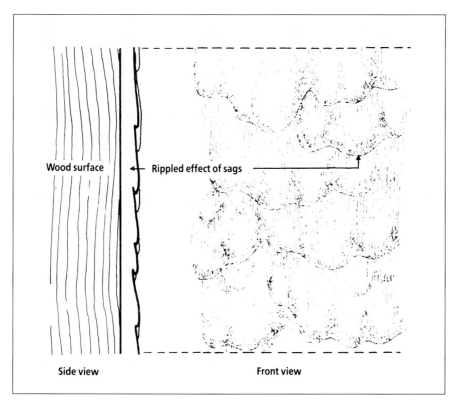

Fig 8.7 Sagging varnish film.

The greatest embarrassment comes when you trap yourself in a room surrounded by wet varnished floor. (This does happen!) Always plan your varnishing so that you start at the point furthest away from the entrance/exit and finish at the point where you can escape. Always close off the room afterwards, to prevent roaming animals and humans increasing your blood pressure. As for ventilation, you will need a little, but do not leave windows wide open, otherwise you will invite dust, leaves and other windblown material to take up permanent residence. And of course the neighbour's cat may leave a pawmark or two as documentary evidence of its visit! (*See* Fig 8.8.)

Heat in the room will aid drying, but do not overheat, as the varnish will go tacky while you are applying it; around 20°C is quite enough. As for the number of coats, this depends to some extent on the manufacturer's recommendation, but high traffic areas will need at least four or five coats. If you have the time and patience, gently hand-sand between coats.

Cork and parquet floors After laying a cork or parquet floor, some time must elapse to allow the adhesive to dry and its solvent to evaporate off; a couple of days should be enough. Instructions for laying these floors include the procedure for cleaning off adhesive from the

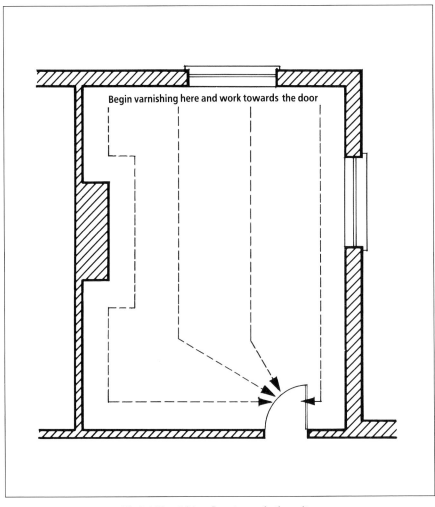

Begin varnishing here and work towards the door

Fig 8.8 Varnishing floor towards the exit.

surface. Always brush the floor prior to varnishing. The first coat of varnish can be thinned with the appropriate solvent (white spirit or water, depending on the type used), up to 10%. Subsequent coats are applied unthinned.

It is a purely personal preference, but floors tend to look better if they are varnished matt or semi-matt; such a finish is also less slippery. Runners and mats laid on the floor should be made non-slip with double-sided tape.

Cork floors should never be sanded, as the material is rather thin, but parquet can be machine-sanded. Always use a belt sander and a medium belt, followed by a fine one. Vacuum clean the floor afterwards to remove as much dust as possible, and allow a couple of days or so for the airborne dust to settle before using the vacuum cleaner again, prior to varnishing.

Floorboards The gaps between old floorboards should be filled with wedges of wood for two reasons: first, the gaps are a source of draughts;

second, small objects and liquids may fall between them into the cavity below. Fig 8.9 shows how the gaps are wedged. They should be left proud until the glue has dried and then planed flush. The boards can be sanded and stained afterwards, if required.

Maintaining a varnished floor is not difficult, although dressing with wax is not recommended. Nothing more than damp dusting will be needed, unless it is heavily soiled. As soon as any wear begins to show, wash the floor, sand it lightly to create a key, and put on a couple of coats of varnish. If it is allowed to deteriorate too much, you may have no option but to strip and begin the process of varnishing all over again. It therefore pays to attack wear as it becomes noticeable.

A traditional recipe for reviving 'tired' floors is a 50/50 mixture of white vinegar and paraffin. Shake the mixture to emulsify it and apply sparingly with a cloth, finally buffing to bring up the finish.

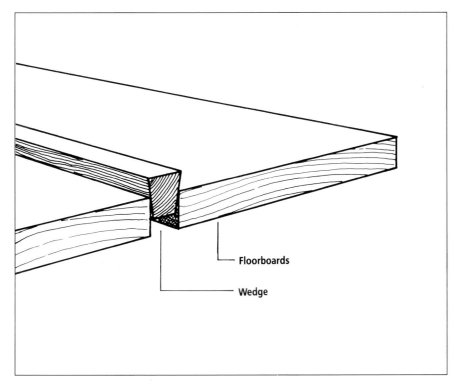

Fig 8.9 Wedging gaps between floorboards.

CHAPTER 9

Modern Synthetic Lacquers

raditional finishes do not lend themselves very well to the rigours of modern mass production methods; they are all relatively labour-intensive, or are simply not durable enough. If stains and polishes can be sprayed on, then time is reduced and turnover increased, but only if the materials are fast-drying. The puzzling thing is that modern methods and materials have acquired a reputation of inferiority when compared with traditional methods and materials; there is a commonly held view that the modern does not have the tradition of craftsmanship. In short, if you spray it on the wood, the 'human' element must have been removed. The truth is that the application of a modern synthetic lacquer requires great skill and technical knowledge. As for the materials themselves, there is a great deal to commend them.

Much money is spent on research and development by companies specializing in the manufacture of finishing materials, and they all rely on the ingenuity of industrial chemists. The range of products available is staggering, and is the response to demands of the furniture industry, who want their furniture to look good when it is sold and to remain that way for a long time, but, at the same time, to be quick to produce. Many of these finishes are available to the amateur in relatively small quantities (5 litres upwards), but you will need to seek out local specialist suppliers. If you contact one or two of the manufacturers listed at the end of the book, they should be able to guide you to stockists, or even supply direct on a mail order basis. You will, of course, need to buy or hire spraying equipment, and more will be said about this later.

We are likely to see some dramatic changes over the next few years because of the Control of Substances Hazardous to Health (COSHH) regulations, which were introduced under the umbrella of the Health and Safety at Work Act, 1974, and which came into force on 1 October 1989. They are designed to reinforce the law concerning the exposure of employees to poten-

tially dangerous materials. As far as the finishing trades are concerned, they mostly relate to solvents and certain other toxic materials, such as isocyanates and general overspray material. In the future, some of the results of the research and development that have gone into finding suitable new finishes conforming to these regulations will filter down the market.

TYPES OF LACQUERS

The early lacquers were relatively crude materials. Today, the market demands higher specifications for wood finishes, and highly sophisticated formulations have resulted. Even so, it is possible to categorize all lacquers into one of the following groups:

- Nitrocellulose (N/C) lacquers.
- Precatalysed (P/C) lacquers.
- Acid-catalysed (A/C) lacquers.

The decision about which lacquer to use should be based on a number of considerations, the main ones being:

- Ease and economy of application.
- Consistent quality and reproducibility.
- Utility.
- Product range (of colours and finishes, i.e. gloss, semi-matt, matt).

It is fair to say that the first and second of these do not present particular problems for the user, as manufacturers of industrial quality finishes are well aware of the need for cost-effectiveness. They are also designed with the large furniture manufacturer in mind, which means that considerable efforts are made to ensure that quality is maintained.

The concept of utility is concerned with the suitability of a lacquer for a specific purpose.

Technical data sheets are produced by manufacturers for each product, and these should be asked for when writing off for product lists and prices. Without this information it is difficult to know the best methods of application, thinning rates, and the appropriate applications.

Lacquers can be obtained in clear or pigmented forms, and as gloss, satin or matt finishes, and from that point there is little to choose between different manufacturers.

What follows is an outline description of the main categories of lacquer, but, as already indicated, you must be guided by the makers' data sheets.

Nitrocellulose Cellulose is a naturally occurring plant material, and N/Cs are derived from this. In many ways it is similar to French polish, in that it is not particularly durable, so its use in industry is now limited. Certainly, none of the major furniture manufacturers would use it because of its poor mechanical properties.

Woodturners and other craftsmen concerned with making 'small' items will find these lacquers useful. They are relatively cheap, very fast-drying, and can be hand-finished to produce a high quality surface, using a process called 'pull-over', which involves some of the technique of using the French polish rubber. Pullover will be described in more detail later.

Commercial furniture makers, from the single craftsman to the mass producer, would not normally consider N/C lacquers as suitable for their purposes: they require a finish with more durability. The larger manufacturer will also be concerned with the problems of storage and transportation, and the attendant risk of damage.

Precatalysed Most wood finishes harden in a very simple way – by drying. Finishing materials are normally solutions of a solid in a solvent; as the solvent evaporates, it leaves the solid component behind. The more concentrated the solution, the thicker the layer of solid left behind –

the so-called 'build'. There is no chemical process involved at all.

By the very nature of the process, if a polish hardens by evaporation of solvent, it can be softened again by application of the same solvent. In other words, they are reversible; this property is useful, should the need for stripping and renewal arise, but it does mean that the finish is not particularly durable either. There are many occasions where a tougher, irreversible finish is needed.

Precatalysed lacquers work by drying, through solvent evaporation, and then by 'curing', i.e. hardening by a chemical reaction called 'polymerization'. During manufacture, a catalyst is added to the lacquer: this is a chemical agent which promotes a chemical reaction but is not chemically active itself in the reaction. While the lacquer remains in its container the catalyst is not active, but as soon as it forms a thin film over the substrate on contact with the air, the chemical process begins. Over a period of several hours after initial drying, the lacquer film undergoes the chemical change by reacting with the air. The resulting lacquer film is made of a different, tougher, chemical than the original.

During the initial stages, pullover can be used to burnish the polish to a high gloss, but after a short period it will not work, because polymerization has begun to change the nature of the chemical.

It is not difficult to realise from the above that precatalysed lacquers have rather better mechanical properties of resistance to moisture, many solvents and, to some degree, heat and scuffing. Precatalysed lacquers usually present some resistance to strippers, and it is often necessary to make several attempts before they work.

Acid-catalysed Again we are dealing with a finish that hardens by chemical reaction brought about by a catalyst. In this case, though, the lacquer and catalyst are not mixed at the manufacturing stage, as the lacquer has a short pot life once the catalyst is added. For this reason, these lacquers are called 'two-pack' products.

Before use, the catalyst is added to the unthinned lacquer and mixed well, prior to thinning for the spray gun. The ratio of catalyst to lacquer is crucial, and the instructions concerning mixing ratios must be adhered to – the speed of curing and the ultimate performance of the lacquer will depend upon it.

It takes a few days for the polish to cure completely, but once fully cured it provides a very tough finish that will resist heat, water and solvents, making it ideal for table tops of all kinds. It is now widely used in the furniture industry, as it is not only good for the customer who wants an easy-care surface, but it is also beneficial to the manufacturer who needs to store and transport the product in pristine condition.

THINNING LACQUERS

Lacquers are sold in a slightly concentrated form and will need to be thinned prior to use, although if you are using a pressure-fed system, this may not be necessary. As a general rule of thumb, thin lacquers with about 20% of the appropriate thinners (i.e. four parts lacquer to one part thinners). Individual equipment, environments and lacquers will have some bearing, so stick to the recommendations provided in the technical literature. In cold or humid conditions, use special anti-bloom thinners in a proportion of about 10%: these reduce the risk of blooming, the formation of a milky-white cast caused by moisture becoming trapped in the wet lacquer.

Manufacturers' technical data refer to thinning in a way that may seem strange: they refer to 'viscosity', a measure of the thickness of the liquid. The higher the viscosity, the thicker the liquid. The viscosity of a lacquer is determined using a viscosity cup (a Ford No. 4 cup – *see* Fig

9.1), which has a known volume and an accurately sized aperture at the bottom. It is filled with the lacquer, which is then allowed to drain from the aperture. The time taken for the cup to drain as a continuous flow is a measure of the viscosity; timing the flow stops when the stream begins to break up. Manufacturers specify the viscosity required for spraying by referring to this time; for example, a lacquer may be specified as requiring a viscosity of 30 seconds, in which case it needs to be thinned so that it flows continuously from the viscosity cup for 30 seconds.

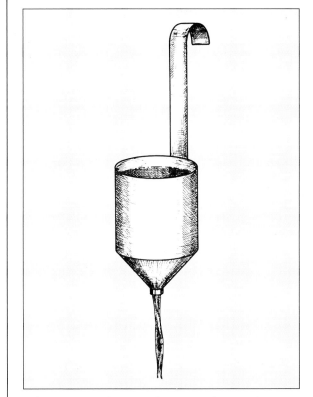

Fig 9.1 No. 4 Ford cup, used to measure lacquer viscosity.

SOLVENTS AND HEALTH AND SAFETY

All the materials so far described in this chapter are based on powerful solvents which are hazardous to health if the operator is not adequately protected. They also represent a fire or explosion risk. Chapter 3 discusses this in more detail; suffice it to say that extreme care must be exercised in the use of these materials. Manufacturers also help by supplying health and safety data for each of their products.

The flammability of these products is measured by flash point, which is the temperature at which a vapour and air mixture will ignite. (Refer to Chapter 3 for more information.)

Much of the risk can be eliminated by the use of spray booths. These range in sophistication from a simple cubicle with an extraction fan, to whole rooms complete with extraction and air conditioning systems. There are essentially two types of cubicle booth – dry back and water-washed (*see* Fig 9.2).

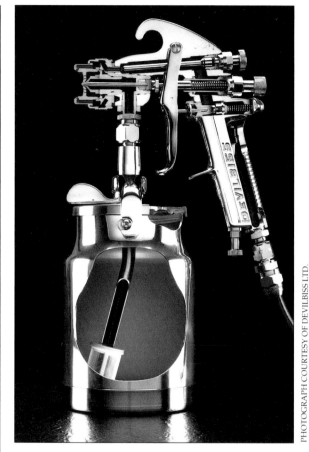

PHOTOGRAPH COURTESY OF DEVILBISS LTD.

Fig 9.3 Spray gun anatomy.

PHOTOGRAPH COURTESY OF BINKS-BULLOWS LTD.

Fig 9.2 Water-washed spray booth.

Dry back Spraying produces considerable wastage of materials, in the form of a fine atomized overspray. The booth confines this cloud in a small area, and an extractor fan draws through a gentle stream of air into the booth and carries the overspray away through a vent at the back of the booth.

Water-washed This is a much more sophisticated system, whereby a constant stream of water runs down the back of the booth; the powdery overspray is caught in the stream and carried away into separation tanks.

SPRAYING EQUIPMENT

In the overwhelming majority of instances, modern synthetic lacquers are sprayed on to the substrate; the solvents upon which most lacquers are based are highly volatile, which makes it difficult to apply them any other way. Some lacquers are specially formulated for brush application, but while this may be appropriate for woodturners or the finishing of small items, it is not suitable for the fine finishing of furniture.

Spray equipment delivers the lacquer with some force as a mist of fine droplets, a process called atomization. If everything goes well, the droplets adhere to the substrate, fuse together and flow into a full and even film. The nozzle, or air cap, of the spray gun is responsible for atomizing the lacquer by forcing it through a narrow aperture. There are two ways in which this process takes place: air atomization and airless atomization.

AIR ATOMIZATION

The basic principle is that a jet of compressed air is mixed with a stream of lacquer, causing it to atomize. This process occurs in a spray gun.

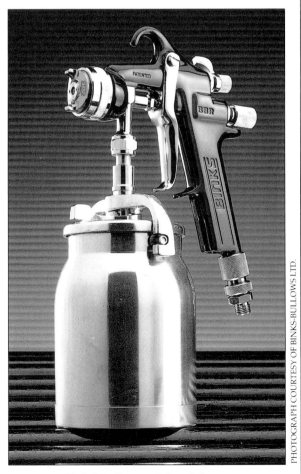

Fig 9.4 Suction- or siphon-fed gun.

PHOTOGRAPH COURTESY OF BINKS-BULLOWS LTD.

Spray Guns

Fig 9.3 shows the basic anatomy of a gun. The air and lacquer become mixed at the cap (nozzle), but there are three ways in which the lacquer may be delivered to the nozzle: suction, gravity feed, or by pressure.

Suction The lacquer is held in a container (called a cup) attached beneath the gun. Air escaping at the cap creates a vacuum immediately in front of it, which siphons the lacquer from the cup. These guns are referred to as siphon-fed (*see* Fig 9.4).

Gravity feed The cup is attached above the body of the gun, allowing gravity to assist the

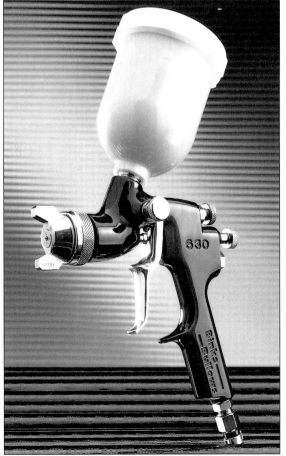

Fig 9.5 Gravity-fed gun.

PHOTOGRAPH COURTESY OF BINKS-BULLOWS LTD.

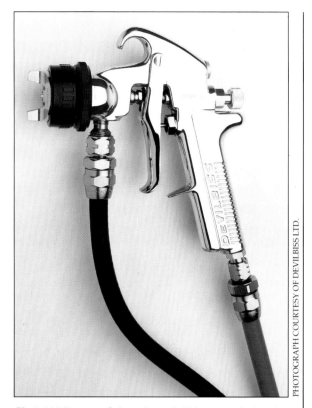

Fig 9.6 (a) Pressure-fed gun has a fluid hose attached to the body of the gun, the lacquer being fed under low pressure (approx 10 psi).

flow of lacquer to the cap. This arrangement allows for a high degree of fine tuning of the spray pattern, which makes the tool ideal for small touching-up jobs and for special effects (shading, speckling, etc.), as well as being a good general-purpose gun (*see* Fig 9.5).

Pressure feed For production runs, a high volume of lacquer will need to be fed to the gun. The material is held in a container some distance away from the gun and supplied to it under pressure provided by air, which is fed separately into the container. Apart from the fact that you do not need to constantly refill a low capacity cup, this system of lacquer delivery is ideal for heavier-bodied lacquers. Suction and gravity-fed systems will usually require lacquers to be thinned with appropriate solvents, but this is often unnecessary with pressure-fed guns, so each pass of the gun over the substrate deposits a heavier film of lacquer. Fig 9.6(a) shows a pressure-fed gun, where the lacquer is delivered to the gun via a pressure hose, while Fig 9.6(b) illustrates the components of such a system.

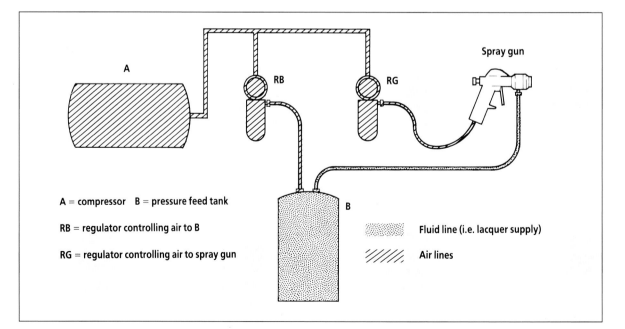

A = compressor B = pressure feed tank

RB = regulator controlling air to B

RG = regulator controlling air to spray gun

Fluid line (i.e. lacquer supply)

Air lines

Fig 9.6 (b) The components of a pressure-fed spray system. The lacquer containers are made in a variety of sizes starting from 2 litres, and air from the compressor is fed into it to maintain the pressurized feed to the gun.

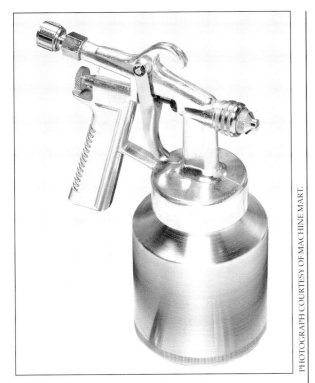

PHOTOGRAPH COURTESY OF MACHINE MART.

Fig 9.7 Small DIY spray kit.

The business end of a spray gun is called the air cap: this directs compressed air into the stream of lacquer to atomize it. Its own performance is affected greatly by the fluid tip and needle as they meter and direct the lacquer into the air stream; together, the cap, needle and tip are called a 'nozzle combination'. It is possible to fit different nozzles to the gun to suit a range of circumstances, and manufacturers' catalogues often contain tables to help you select the most appropriate nozzle. The choice depends upon:

■ What is available for your model of gun.

■ The type and viscosity (thickness) of the lacquer.

■ The rate at which air is supplied to the gun from the compressor, in cubic feet per minute (cfm) or litres per minute (l/m), and the air pressure, measured in pounds per square inch (psi) or bars.

Atomization occurs when the compressed air comes into contact with the stream of lacquer; this can take place on either the inside or the outside of the cap.

Internal mix Where low air volume and pressures are involved, the gun is usually designed to mix the air and lacquer inside the cap before expelling them. These guns are typical of those supplied with DIY kits – Fig 9.7 shows such an outfit for the DIY enthusiast. They are not designed for extended periods of use, and are not usually employed where high quality finishing is required.

External mix The lacquer passes through the aperture of the cap, and is then atomized by jets of compressed air directed into it outside the cap. This type of gun is designed more for

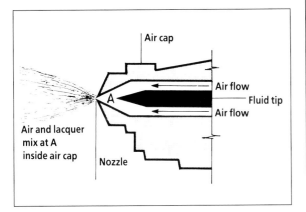

Fig 9.8 (a) Design of an internal mix cap.

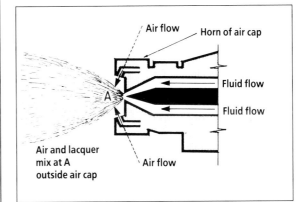

Fig 9.8 (b) Design of an external mix cap.

Fig 9.9 Portable compressor unit.

professional use, and will produce high quality finishes. These guns have higher air consumption and pressures, and need higher capacity air compressors.

Fig 9.8 shows the anatomy of internal and external mix caps.

Compressors

As with spray guns, the choice of compressor is a matter of horses for courses. Their motors may be electrically driven or powered by internal combustion: a compressor may be rated according to the power of the motor or, more usefully, by the rate at which it can supply air, i.e. 8cfm at 50psi.

Another important point to consider is whether the compressor has an air receiver and if so, its volume (i.e. a tank which will store the compressed air at high pressure – around 150psi). The small DIY units frequently do not

have a receiver, so air is supplied to the gun directly from the compressor unit. The value of the receiver is that it ensures the gun has a constant supply of air, without fluctuations in pressure or volume flow.

Fig 9.9 shows a compressor unit suitable for use with a single gun. It is vital to match the gun to the compressor, as the latter must be capable of supplying air at the rate required by the gun's nozzle. It is pointless running a gun whose nozzle requires 10cfm at 50psi, if the compressor can only supply 6cfm at 50psi – the gun will simply run out of air! As a general rule, the compressor should be rated higher than the air consumption required by the gun.

Air Regulator/Filter

The pressure of the air in the receiver must be reduced before delivery to the gun. It must also be clear of any contaminants, as these would be carried on to the substrate with the atomized lacquer. The main contaminants are water vapour, oil from the motor, and dust.

In the portable compressor shown in Fig 9.9, a pressure switch operates when the pressure in the receiver reaches 150psi, and air leaving it for the gun will pass through the regulator/filter arrangement shown. Its function is to reduce the pressure of the air to the gun to that required (such as 50psi), and the filter removes all the contaminants at the same time. Note that there are also two gauges: one reads the reservoir pressure, the other the line pressure, the pressure of the air delivered to the gun. This latter pressure can be adjusted to suit the particular requirements of the job.

AIRLESS ATOMIZATION

In airless systems, atomization is achieved by pumping the lacquer to the gun nozzle under high pressure and forcing it through the nozzle,

Fig 9.10 (a) A small DIY airless spray gun.

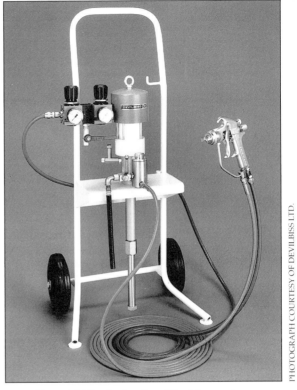

Fig 9.10 (b) Professional quality airless system.

so that it breaks up into the atomized mist. Fig 9.10 illustrates two types: (a) a small DIY unit, and (b) a professional airless unit.

In general, airless systems do not produce the quality of finish that can be obtained through air atomization, and so would not normally be recommended for finishing. On the other hand, air systems generate a good deal of waste, as some of the lacquer is oversprayed, while airless units generate less overspray.

SPRAYING TECHNIQUE

This starts by understanding the operation of the gun: there are two controls, one for the rate of flow of lacquer to the nozzle, the other to control the distribution of the lacquer as it leaves the gun, ranging from a pencil spray to a flat, wide fan. The air pressure is controlled at the compressor. In general, the wider the fan, the

more lacquer you will need to flow to the nozzle to maintain a good spray pattern. The trick is to coordinate pressure, fan and material flow so that just the right amount of lacquer reaches the wood to give a good, full coat, one which doesn't run. Virtually all the problems associated with learning the technique revolve around this; the thing to do is to set the pressure at 50psi and fiddle around with flow and fan to create the ideal spray pattern, as shown in Fig 9.11. Before spraying any lacquer on to wood, practise on scrap wood first to get the pattern right.

The spraying distance should be 8in–10in (20.3cm–25.4cm) from the work; do not vary this during any one coating. Always keep the gun moving while lacquer is leaving the gun, and keep it parallel to the work; any arcing will cause uneven coating. Work along the grain (this also helps as a reference), and make each pass of the gun overlap the last by 50% (*see* Fig 9.12): this will ensure that a full even coat is applied.

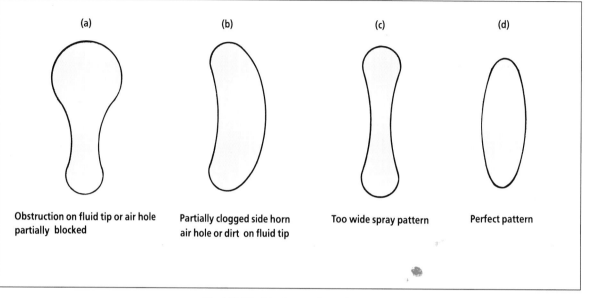

(a) Obstruction on fluid tip or air hole partially blocked

(b) Partially clogged side horn air hole or dirt on fluid tip

(c) Too wide spray pattern

(d) Perfect pattern

Fig 9.11 The ideal spray fan pattern.

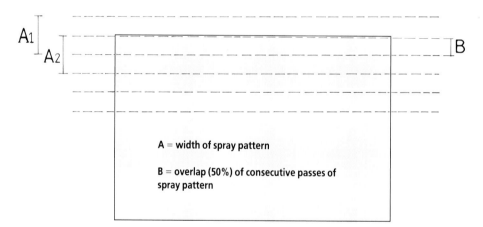

A = width of spray pattern

B = overlap (50%) of consecutive passes of spray pattern

Fig 9.12 The overlap of each pass of the spray gun should be about 50%.

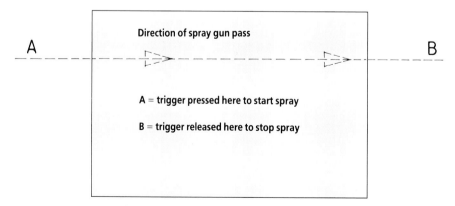

Direction of spray gun pass

A = trigger pressed here to start spray

B = trigger released here to stop spray

Fig 9.13 The trigger action to ensure even application of lacquer.

An important part of the skill is the trigger action, which is in two steps. As you depress the trigger, the air is first turned on, and as you depress further, the lacquer flow to the nozzle is activated. It is vitally important that spraying is done in this order: each pass should start before the gun reaches the surface, and end after it has passed the other side (*see* Fig 9.13); in this way there will be no sudden heavy deposits as the gun is switched on, or dry areas as it is turned off.

WORKING PROCEDURE

The working environment is important: the air should be warm and dry (around 25°C), to aid drying and prevent blooming. Do not use naked flames or incandescent elements during and after spraying.

Surface Preparation

The initial preparation of the substrate is the same as for any other finish. Chapter 4 outlines the procedures in some detail, but should imperfections require filling with stopping, be careful, as the powerful solvents found in lacquers may not be compatible with the stopping material – for example, the surface of shellac stopping may be softened. To prevent this, special cellulose-based stoppings should be used – these can be bought from the same supplier as the lacquer.

Stain

There is always a hidden danger with staining, in that if powerful solvents are used in the finish, they may dissolve and lift the stain out of the surface of the wood, giving rise to a very patchy effect. Water-based stains are safe to use, but oil stains may lead to such a problem.

Chapter 5 describes the nature of stains and goes into some detail on industrial stain materials. The main point is that the lacquer manufacturer will also produce stains that can be used safely beneath the lacquer. Because they are intended for industrial use, the formulation makes them fast-drying, and the idea is to spray them on as a full wet coat and allow them to dry. Once a full coat has been sprayed on, it is possible to wipe over the surface with a rag to even out the colour. On small areas there is no overriding reason why the stain cannot be applied by brush or pad as described in Chapter 5, although you would need to work quickly because of the speed of drying. These stains are normally ready to be sprayed over after about an hour.

Grain Filling

As in French polishing, this is optional, and depends on whether or not you want a full- or open-grain effect. Special cream fillers can be bought for use under cellulose lacquers, and you should use the same brand of filler as the lacquer.

To ensure compatibility, always buy the different components of the finishing process from the same manufacturer. The companies provide the necessary information in their brochures, to leave you in no doubt about the compatibility of the different products. Some materials have universal application, while others are specifically designed to be associated with particular products.

Toning

Chapter 10 looks in detail at the general theory and practice of correcting colour errors, but mention needs to be made at this point of the procedure of colour correction in spraying. It is sometimes the case that the colour after staining is not quite right, and a correction needs to be made; this is done by spraying what are known as toners, which are colours sprayed on to the work to modify its colour. For example, a dark oak stain may be too cool (i.e. have a lot of green in it); by spraying on a weak red colour, the whole work can be warmed up. In reproduction work, you may want to simulate light and dark areas, and this can be done by spraying on a darker colour around the edges of panels, for example, to create shading. You will need to use a gravity-fed gun for this, as it will provide better spray control for this type of work.

It is even possible to add powder pigments such as black to the lacquer, to give a general overall wash of translucent colour or darken the whole work. However, it is important to go easy on the pigments, otherwise you will effectively spray an opaque paint on to the work.

This whole process of colouring is highly skilful, and relies on the polisher's colour judgment. This skill is acquired on a 'nature and nurture' basis – it is partly an innate sense as well as a skill acquired through experience.

Sanding Sealer

The work is now sprayed with a coat of sanding sealer. This stage is equivalent to fadding in French polishing, where the aim is to seal the wood, to reduce its suction and provide a smooth base coat for the top coats. You should buy a sanding sealer compatible with the finishing lacquer, i.e. precatalysed sealer for P/C and A/C lacquers, and cellulose sealer for N/C lacquers.

Sanding sealer is simply a lacquer in which is suspended a very fine powder, which makes it heavy-bodied. At the same time, the powder allows abrasive paper to 'bite', making smoothing much easier (the paper tends to clog when sanding lacquers). In a warm environment, the surface can be lightly sanded with 320 grit paper after about 30–40 minutes. Dust off with a tack rag.

Finishing Coats

Two coats will usually be sufficient; allow at least an hour between them, gently denibbing after the first and dusting off with a tack rag. It will be necessary to dust between successive coats, due to the settling-out of some overspray. For matt and satin lacquers, the job is now complete and the work should be set aside to harden for a few days (especially in the case of catalyzed lacquers).

If the lacquer is a gloss N/C, you may wish to improve the finish as described below.

Pullover

The finish straight from the gun may show a slight 'orange peel' effect, even when thinned correctly. Special pullover solvents can be bought which, when applied with a rubber (like French polish), gently soften the surface and 'pull' it flat. Use figure of eight strokes, as in French polishing, followed by straight strokes along the grain. The final finish should resemble a good French-polished surface.

It should be borne in mind that this process is really only effective on N/C lacquers, because the solvents will soften the lacquer surface. A/C and P/C lacquers harden by chemical reaction, and so will not pullover readily, although reasonably good results can be obtained on P/Cs, provided pullover takes place within about two hours of the final application. Pullover can be applied to N/Cs at any time after the final coat has dried.

Burnishing

This should only be carried out on full-grained finishes, as any open grain will trap the burnishing cream and show up as unsightly white flecks.

The lacquer must first be cut back slightly to remove any blemishes, such as the odd speck of dust, using very fine (400–600 grit) wet-or-dry paper used wet, before being wiped clean, allowed to dry and then dusted down.

A burnishing cream contains very mildly abrasive powders, and the consistency is similar to a wax cream. It is applied over the whole surface in straight strokes along the grain with a damp mutton cloth. Keep rubbing over the surface until you can feel that the surface has polished to a high gloss; this is difficult because it is clouded by the cream, but with experience you will develop this feel. Allow the cream to dry on the surface before buffing along the grain with a dry cloth. The surface may look slightly hazy, but this can be removed using a reviver (*see* Chapter 16).

Burnishing should only be carried out on lacquers that have been allowed to harden for at least a couple of days. All types of lacquer can be burnished, but in the cases of P/C and A/C products, where pullover is not all that successful, it is the only way to achieve a mirror finish.

LACQUERING DEFECTS

There are a number of problems that can be experienced when spray lacquering. The following are the most common:

Cissing This manifests itself as pockmarks or small bubbles, and results from either water or oil entering the lacquer spray. The source is the compressor itself, and cissing indicates a filter that is either faulty or in need of cleaning. The filter should be drained after each spraying session. The only cure for cissing is stripping and starting again.

Orange peel The name aptly describes the surface effect, where it has the texture of orange peel. This is the result of under-thinning or too heavy a coat. The surface can be rubbed down before respraying, but there is often still residual orange peel, and it is better to either pullover, or, failing that, strip and respray.

Blooming If the surface develops a milky white appearance, moisture has become trapped in the lacquer film. The causes are a cold, damp atmosphere where, as the solvent evaporates, the surface cools down to below the dew point of water, and air moisture condenses out on to the wet lacquer; or there may be moisture in the wood, perhaps after stripping. It may burnish out, but otherwise strip and respray.

Granular texture A very common result for the inexperienced sprayer, caused by either having the gun too far away from the surface or by using too fast a pass. Either way, insufficient lacquer is put on to the wood to produce a full film; when you run your hand over it, the surface feels like fine abrasive paper. Rub down and respray.

Tackiness A thick film of lacquer may skin over, trapping wet lacquer beneath and preventing the solvent from evaporating. It can take two or three days for the film to dry. The only thing you can do is wait and keep the atmosphere warm. The effect shows itself as patches that clearly look wet and will show fingerprints if touched.

If an acid-catalysed lacquer has been used, it could be that not enough catalyst was added; all you can do is wait until it dries completely in a warm environment.

Spitting This is more a problem within the gun, where grit, oil or water has managed to enter the mechanism, interrupting the airflow. The remedy is to clean out the gun and, if necessary, disassemble the compressor filter and clean it with cellulose thinners, to remove excess oil. In any case, the filter should be drained after each job: an easy matter, as filters are fitted with a draining point.

CHAPTER 10

Colouring

obody is perfect – there are times when you have applied great care and skill, but things still go wrong.

One of the most difficult areas of woodfinishing is colour: it occasionally happens that the stain you applied appeared to be the right colour until you started polishing. The change that takes place can sometimes be quite striking, and there are two basic reasons for this: first, the polish itself may be coloured, and will add its own cast to the wood's colour; the other main cause for colour change is the way light is reflected from the surface. Polish changes light's reflective characteristics, and so apparently changes its appearance.

On the other hand, you may simply have made a mistake! For instance, mahogany stains are frequently rather red, and when used on mahogany itself, this redness becomes quite fiery and may need toning down. This highlights the care that needs to be taken when choosing a stain; take the colour of the wood itself into account. This illustrates the need for testing the colour of a stain on a piece of timber from the same batch used for the work being polished. Having said all this, we all occasionally need to lock the stable door after the horse has bolted, and the purpose of this chapter is to look at the techniques of making the necessary corrections.

Another problem is the difference between areas of the work. Wood is not an homogeneous material; it varies tremendously in terms of colour, porosity and figuring, and staining alone will not produce an even hue. If the work you are finishing exhibits the sort of variations just described, the process of colouring may be needed to create uniformity – if that is what you want or need. Allied to this is the problem of colour-matching repaired patches to the original, surrounding area.

This chapter is concerned with correcting colour problems during French polishing or varnishing. Chapter 9 is concerned with modern synthetic lacquers, and their colour correction is dealt with in that chapter, but the general principles behind the relationships between colours remain the same.

Correcting a colour cast is a tricky process, and one in which you need to have a good and thorough understanding of how light and colour behave. For example, it is only by knowing how colours interact with each other that using a 'wash' of green stain or polish to correct a fiery red cast becomes the obvious solution.

THE COLOUR SPECTRUM AND COLOUR VISION

The phenomenon of the colours of the rainbow was taught to us all at some point or other, with prisms and rays of light passing through them, projecting the seven colours on to a screen. For most people, the ability to see those colours and to distinguish between them is something that can be taken for granted. However, anyone with a colour vision problem will find this type of work rather difficult.

At this point, we could become involved in the philosophical argument, do we really see what we appear to see and, more importantly, do others see it in exactly the same way as us? There have been occasions where I have been

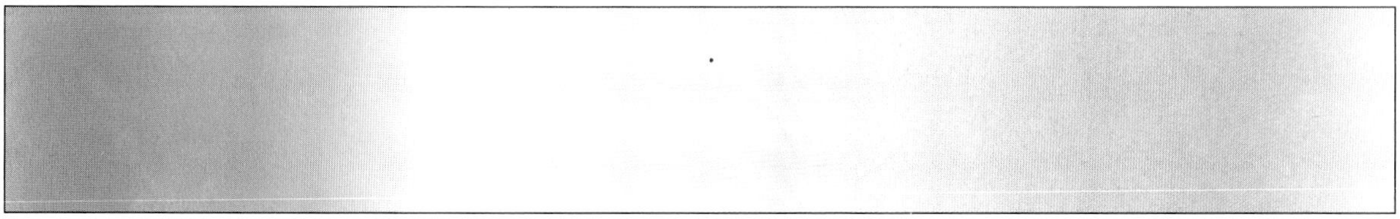

Fig 10.1 The colour spectrum.

Behaviour of Light

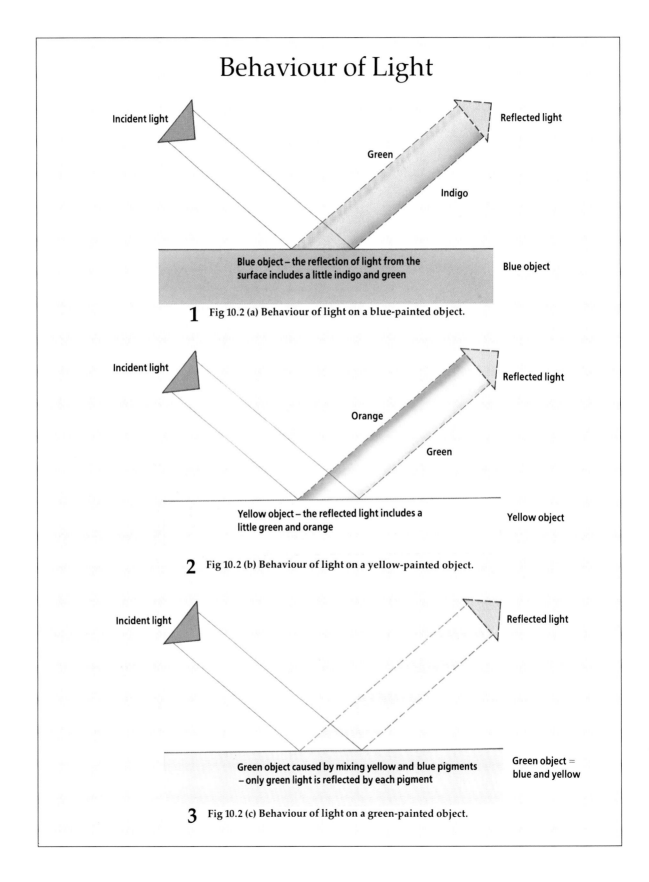

1 Fig 10.2 (a) Behaviour of light on a blue-painted object.

2 Fig 10.2 (b) Behaviour of light on a yellow-painted object.

3 Fig 10.2 (c) Behaviour of light on a green-painted object.

aware of a difference in colour, while someone else does not seem to perceive the difference at all. The reverse situation has also occurred. It is all very contentious at times, and while I do not want to dwell on this point, it should be borne in mind as an area of work that promises to 'bite back' from time to time, and may lead to some disagreement.

Fig 10.1 is a reminder of the colour spectrum, and shows the colours as they are represented conventionally, from red through to violet. The order aids understanding of how our eyes and brains perceive colours when dyes and pigments are mixed.

Fig 10.2(a) represents a blue-painted object. When light falls upon it, some is reflected and the rest is absorbed by the object. The material reflects its own colour, i.e. blue, and absorbs all the other colours, except for a small amount of the two colours that are adjacent to blue in the spectrum – green and indigo – but we are barely aware of them. Using the same argument, a yellow-painted object will reflect yellow light and absorb all the others, except for a little green and orange (*see* Fig 10.2(b)). The clever bit is when we mix the blue and yellow paints together. Why do we see green? There is no apparent logic for this at all – or is there? When light strikes the new, green object, the blue pigment will attempt to reflect its band of colours (blue, with a little indigo and green), but the yellow pigment will absorb the blue and indigo and attempt to reflect its colour band (yellow, with a little green and orange). The blue pigment will absorb the yellow light and the orange.

It now appears that all the colours have been absorbed by the object's surface bar one – green – which is reflected and is seen by our eyes. Thus by mixing blue and yellow, we arrive at green (*see* Fig 10.2(c)). If this all seems a bit confusing, spend a little time working through and digesting its logic; by understanding the process, you can see the principles behind using some very strange colours to correct errors.

THE COLOUR TRIANGLE

Fig 10.3 shows the colour triangle. This is based on the principle of mixing colours we learned at primary school. In theory, if all the primary colours are mixed together, we should end up with black, because all the light would be absorbed and none would be reflected. In practice, this does not happen because coloured pigments are imperfect so some light does become reflected, which leads to the familiar muddy hue.

We can use the colour triangle to work out how to correct an unwanted colour cast. For example, how can we correct too red a shade, or even warm up a cold green-brown oak stain? These are two common enough problems that the woodfinisher may be faced with. Perhaps the colour is almost a perfect match with another item – but not quite. The colour triangle can again help in determining the appropriate correction.

The points of the triangle represent the primary colours (blue, red and yellow). The sides represent the colours produced when the primary colours adjacent to it are mixed. In the centre you can see an area of neutrality – where no particular colour seems to be present – this is

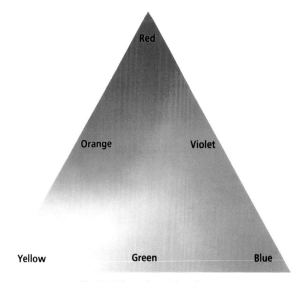

Fig 10.3 The colour triangle.

the result of all three primary colours being mixed. A colour cast is corrected by applying the colour opposite to it in the triangle. For example, red is neutralized by green, yellow by purple, etc.

COLOUR CORRECTION

One of the commonest errors is to create a mahogany, or even an oak or walnut, that is too red. According to the colour triangle, this can be toned down by using a coat of green, taking care not to overdo things by making the green too strong; begin with a very weak colour.

How you go about the process of correction depends upon the finish concerned. The manufacturers of spray lacquers produce toning colours that can be mixed with the lacquer and sprayed over the offending surface almost like a colour wash.

If you are French polishing, a little spirit aniline dye can be mixed with transparent polish. The surface is then polished in the usual way with a rubber until the desired correction is achieved.

It is tempting to use a strong colour in the belief that this will have the desired effect quicker. This is not so, however, and all that happens is that you replace one problem with another by creating another undesirable hue. By using a very weak colour and successive, thin applications, there will be a gradual approach to neutralizing the cast. You simply apply as many coats as required: the first application may not produce any really noticeable effect, but the second and any subsequent applications should demonstrate a considerable change.

Varnishing presents a more difficult problem, as very few dyes will dissolve in the solvents (unless water-based varnishes are used, in which case water-based aniline dyes are ideal). The very nature of varnishing also means that relatively thick coats are applied, so there is always the danger of overcolouring. In many cases the answer is to prepare some spirit aniline dye and mix it with a little transparent French polish, applying the resulting mixture with a rubber. When the colour is satisfactory you can continue varnishing normally.

Unfortunately, photographs cannot show the effect of colouring satisfactorily, so you must take it on trust that using what seem to be 'unconventional' colours to correct unwanted casts does actually work. If you examine the colour triangle and use your own knowledge of colour mixing, the reasoning behind it is quite sound.

Fiery red is not the only colour cast to cause a problem. Some dark oak stains have a heavy green bias, which gives the work a rather cold appearance. The greenish, cold oak can be warmed up by colouring with red, while the orange cast can be rectified with blue. Again, the colour triangle shows why. But remember to always use a very weak colour – or else!

THE COLOURING PROCEDURE

When does colouring take place? In theory, any time after staining. In practice, it is often better to tackle the problem after the first coat of polish has been applied, as it is only at this point that you will have some real idea of the final colour. By applying an effective sealing coat, any mistakes made in the colour can usually be reversed, for example by stripping and starting again. Colour applied directly on to a stained, but as yet unsealed, surface may create problems as the dye sinks into the wood.

Another useful tip is to make a pattern. Many items to be coloured can be divided into a number of different parts, or perhaps even physically disassembled for the purpose of polishing. Where this is the case, take one of those parts, i.e. a table top or a drawer front, 'colour it down' to the correct hue, and use it as a pattern – your reference colour, to which all the other parts must be matched.

Finally, if more than one application of colour is needed, always allow more than adequate time for complete drying of the previous coats. If you do not, there is the very real danger of 'lifting' the colour and causing patchiness.

GENERAL DARKENING

A stain is frequently the right colour when applied to the wood; but when you begin to polish, it becomes obvious that, while the colour is more or less correct, it may not be dark enough. You will need to darken the surface without changing the basic colour: for this you should use pigments rather than dyes.

Stains based on dyes are relatively transparent, and the aim of darkening polish is to give it an opacity which effectively darkens it. Pigments do not dissolve in any of the polishes that a woodfinisher uses, and so will have an obliterating effect. For darkening, you will need to make up a 'darkening polish': mix a little vegetable black pigment in the polish, ensuring that it is completely dispersed. Add a little reddish pigment (i.e. burnt sienna) to this mixture and completely disperse it. This should produce a slightly muddy brown.

Guidance on exact quantities of pigment cannot be given, as this depends upon individual circumstances. The colour balance of the darkening polish will be determined by the amount of darkening required: sometimes the balance needs to be towards the red, and sometimes towards the black. This may not sound terribly helpful; however, this is not an exact science, but very much a subjective art! Experience very definitely improves your skill, and a highly developed colour sense will prove to be invaluable.

The same rule about depth of colour applies: the darkening polish must not look like a paint, i.e. so heavily laden with pigment that it is a solid colour. It must still be fairly transparent because, again, you achieve the end result by applying it in thin coats. If there is too much pigment, the polish will dry as a solid obliterating coat, and will be quite rough. Lacquer can be sprayed, while French polish and varnish should be laid on to the work in thin coats, using a fad (*see* Chapter 7). Allow plenty of drying time between coats.

Fig 10.4 illustrates a before and after effect.

PAINTING OUT BLEMISHES

Fig 10.5 shows the sort of blemish that should be corrected using the painting-out technique. This ring in a French-polished surface was caused by a glass or cup with a wet base; in most cases, white ring marks result from moisture entering

Fig 10.4 The effect of a 'darkening' polish.

the polish film and discolouring it. The technique for repairing these blemishes is described in Chapter 13, but this case is somewhat different, in that the polish has been taken off the wood altogether and must be repaired with a colouring polish.

Fig 10.6 shows the various stages.

1 The light area is stained to bring it close to the colour required.

2 The process of darkening begins by making up a darkening polish. Here, the colour balance is towards black, and there is a little more pigment mixed in the polish, so it is more opaque. The colour is 'painted' on to the blemish using a very fine artist's brush (perhaps a 00): note that very short strokes are used so that the colour does not appear as great blotches.

3 Finally, the short strokes begin to overlap and give the appearance of grain texture, totally masking the blemish. When the polish has dried, the whole surface is given a few coats of French polish to complete the restoration process.

A more difficult case of painting out is shown in Fig 10.7. Cigarette burns are a real challenge: it is difficult, maybe impossible, to mask the blemish in a way that will not be detected. The choice is very simple: you can leave the blemish – a very ugly scar – or you can reduce its visual impact by painting it out in such a way that the area closely resembles the surrounding surface. Even though it may still be noticeable, painting out may be the better alternative.

Fig 10.8 shows the repaired blemish.

1 The blemish will be masked by overlaying it with different colours. You need to begin by determining which colours to use. Look at the surface and you will see that there is a base colour; this is usually the lightest of them. Mix up your 'paint' in French polish or lacquer (depending on the medium concerned) so that its colour resembles the base colour: you may need more than one pigment to do this. Use a fine artist's brush to lay this colour down with short strokes along the grain. This will hide the blemish, but will leave a definite 'smudge'.

Painting Out Blemishes

1 Fig 10.5 Colour and polish completely removed by a wet object.

2 Fig 10.6 Rectifying the blemish by staining and painting out.

Painting Out Cigarette Burns

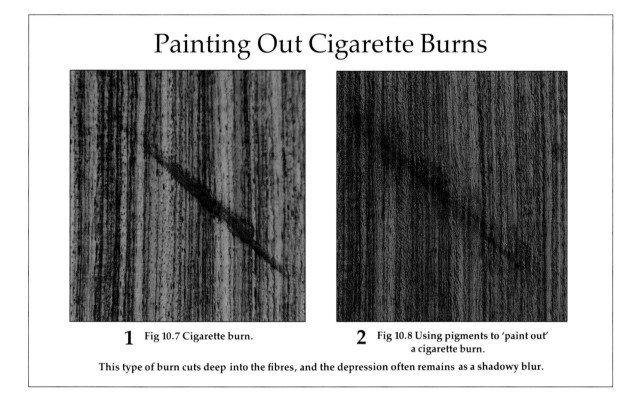

1 Fig 10.7 Cigarette burn.

2 Fig 10.8 Using pigments to 'paint out' a cigarette burn.

This type of burn cuts deep into the fibres, and the depression often remains as a shadowy blur.

2 Next, determine the next lightest colour, make up your paint and brush this on to the patch, after a good drying time has been allowed. You do need to be careful here: the aim is not to cover the whole patch, but to begin simulating the grain texture or figure.

3 There may be other colours that need to be overlaid, and these are done in ascending order of darkness. In other words, you begin the process with the lightest colour and finish with the darkest. You will rarely need more than about three colours. Allow plenty of time for previous coats to dry, and remember that the colours must be laid down with short strokes of the fine artist's brush, and should be in a similar pattern to the real pattern of the figuring. When the process is complete, allow a couple of hours to dry and seal in the colour with a coat of clear polish applied with a rubber (either French polish or lacquer, but without any pressure). If necessary or practical, give the whole surface a coat or two of polish.

Deep scratches are easier to handle. Mix up your paint with slightly less pigment so that it is not so opaque. Colour out the scratch by painting along it (*see* Fig 10.9) before sealing in with polish, also applied by brush, and refinishing the whole surface to blend it in. Because the 'paint' is less opaque, you may need two or three applications.

Fig 10.9 Colouring out a scratch.

CHAPTER 11

Finishing
Turned Work

Lathe-turned wood has its own special needs and properties, and therefore should be examined as a separate item – although many finishing techniques will be familiar.

HOLDING THE WORKPIECE

The main problem in finishing turned work is holding the item. Wherever possible, keep the part to be finished on the lathe: this is quite simple when dealing with between centres turning, but faceplate and chuck work can present some difficulties. Bowl work, in particular, sometimes generates the problem that after turning the outside, the blank is turned around to shape the inside, at which point it can be difficult to have free access to the outside, depending on shape and size. It is a matter of planning ahead, and you may find that it is more practical to polish certain parts of the piece prior to completing the turning – i.e. the outside of the bowl is polished before turning the inside. Each case

must be treated on an individual basis, but in many cases you should be able to delay the finishing process until all the turning has been completed. By keeping the work on the lathe you can keep both hands free, so as not to ruin the finish by handling it.

STAINING

The general trend is towards keeping the work in its natural colour, and allowing the wood's characteristic figure to speak for itself. There are occasions, however, where you may want to stain, for example restoration work where you have no choice but to colour-match. Again, it is better to stain and polish on the lathe and fit afterwards.

This is where you are going to run into problems, as the old stains were principally water-based, and their depth and clarity of colour is difficult to match using modern oil- or spirit-based stains. The problem is that turnings have a very large proportion of short and end

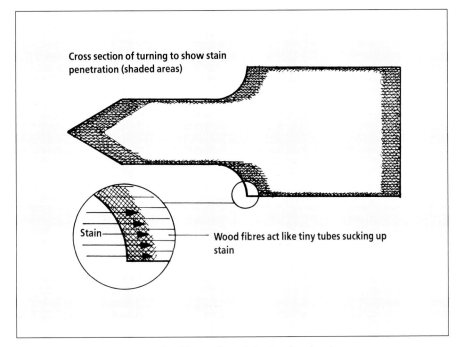

Fig 11.1 Capillary action of short and end grain.

grain, which absorb far more water through capillary action than other areas, causing them to become much darker (*see* Fig 11.1). At the same time, the wood fibres will have been compressed by the machining. As soon as water comes into contact with these fibres, they swell and cause roughness. If water stains have to be used, carry out the grain-raising procedure first, smoothing the work while still on the lathe.

If at all possible, use oil or spirit stains, bearing in mind the problems of incompatibility with the final finish that may arise. (These problems are discussed in Chapter 5.)

FINISHING MATERIALS

The finishes most commonly used by turners are: wax; oil; French polish; cellulose/melamine; two-pack catalysed lacquers.

Wax

If the item is not intended to be handled a great deal or for use with food, waxing is a quick and attractive finish, producing a low lustre that allows the figure of the wood to speak for itself. However, it is not durable, and so will not stand up to much handling; the work will quickly become grubby and lose its initial attraction.

Carnauba is the traditional woodturners' wax; it is bought as a stick or block, and is held against the work as it rotates on the lathe. Friction melts the wax, and by slowly moving the block from one end of the work to the other, it is distributed over the whole surface. The work is then polished by holding wood shavings against the rotating workpiece at slow speed; the friction burnishes the wax to a gloss (*see* Fig 11.2). A final buff with a polishing cloth, with the lathe stopped, tidies it up and removes wood dust.

The problem with carnauba is that it is brittle and can chip off the work. Also, because the block of wax is hard (similar to a block of toffee),

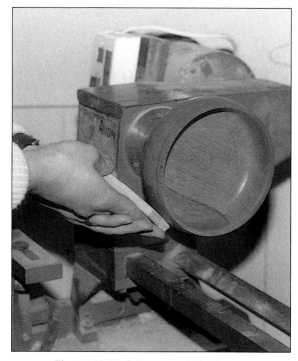

Fig 11.2 (a) Applying carnauba by friction.

soft-textured woods can be damaged by the pressure needed to generate sufficient friction to melt it. A compromise is to use a carnauba/beeswax (50/50 mix) block, which can be bought ready-made; you can make it yourself, using a double boiler to melt the waxes.

The alternative is to use wax polish. Apply it with a cloth to the stationary workpiece (it is very easy to get a cloth trapped on a rotating item), allow to dry and harden for an hour, and polish, using the shavings technique described above. To finish, buff with a clean polishing cloth. Some woods may need one or two more applications.

Some time can be saved if you give the work a coat of sanding sealer first. Sealers are either shellac- or cellulose-based; both contain a quantity of a chemically inert, fine white powder which allows abrasive paper to bite more effectively. By sealing the grain before waxing, you reduce the amount of wax that is needed, and at the same time seal the pores against dirt. The sealer is brushed on to the stationary item with a polish mop or similar soft-haired brush, ensuring that no runs occur or at least go uncorrected (they are very difficult to remove once dry), and allowed to dry for an hour or so. The surface is then denibbed (i.e. the adhering dust particles are removed) using very fine abrasive (320 grit or finer) before waxing.

Oil

Richly figured woods such as walnut and the various burrs look stunning when oiled, and apart from the fact that it is a durable finish, oil helps reduce drying out and cracking.

Any of the oils described in Chapter 6 can be used and applied in the normal way, but expect turned work to be thirstier because of the short and end grain. Apply generously, perhaps with a soft bristled brush, and allow a day to soak in. Burnish with a soft cloth (with the article stationary), and repeat with a second, and possibly third, coat. There is a lot to be said for completely immersing the article in oil for a day or so before removing and wiping off the surplus. After the oil has soaked in, burnish on the lathe at slow speed with shavings (see Fig 11.2(b)). Put the piece to one side for a couple of weeks for the oil to harden. This procedure is valid for proprietary oil polishes as well as linseed.

The proprietary oils are probably better for gaining a good finish quickly, but if the object is to be used with food, you must not use them, or linseed, because they will taint the food; there are also substances in proprietary oils that will contaminate, such as terebene or similar drying agents. These articles must be left unfinished, or an edible vegetable oil can be employed. I always use one of the lighter oils, such as sunflower, safflower or rapeseed, on all turned objects where I use oil polishing; they are so light they soak in rapidly and, being pale, they do not cause an appreciable colour change.

If an object is to be washed regularly, it is pointless applying any finish, as nothing will tolerate that kind of treatment over a long period.

French Polish

The initial coats are best applied with a polishing mop. The material to use is a shellac-based sanding sealer, again watching out for runs. After an hour or so, it can be cut back and another coat applied. Two or three coats will normally be enough to produce a high, grain-filling build, but if not, apply as many coats as necessary.

After cutting back the last coat, make a rubber of suitable size to fit the work and use this to

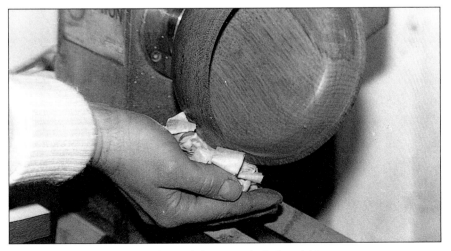

Fig 11.2 (b) Applying carnauba by burnishing.

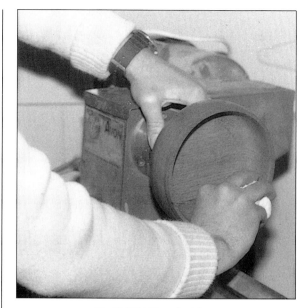

Fig 11.3 (a) Use of rubber.

Fig 11.3 (b) Use of rubber.

build up the gloss with French polish, rotating the work by hand (*see* Fig 11.3).

Sanding sealer is normally a creamy white, but this does not usually matter; you can also dye the sealer with spirit aniline dye of the appropriate colour if necessary. In fact, if staining the wood at all, you can use coloured sealer to build up the colour, and finish off with transparent or garnet French polish in the rubber.

Once the polish has completely hardened for at least 24 hours, it can be burnished to a high gloss with a proprietary burnishing cream or even a little rottenstone or Vienna chalk in linseed oil, applied on a small pad of cotton wool and held against the workpiece as it rotates at low speed (*see* Fig 11.4). Take care not to generate so much heat that the shellac melts and ruins all your hard work.

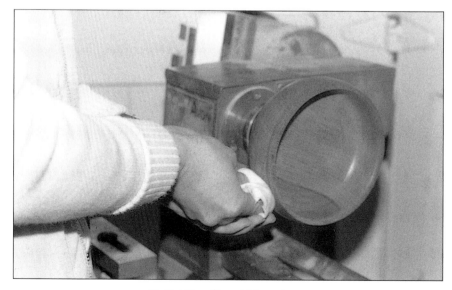

Fig 11.4 Use of burnishing cream.

Fig 11.5 Burnishing with steel wool and wax polish.

Cellulose/Melamine

A number of manufacturers produce fast-drying lacquers based on cellulose and/or melamine, with other synthetic polymers added. They are brushed on, allowed to dry and then cut back. A second coat is applied and allowed to harden before burnishing with a pad of steel wool lubricated with a little wax polish, while the lathe rotates at its slowest speed. It is best to allow the second coat to harden for several hours (*see* Fig 11.5). The work is then hand-buffed with the lathe stationary.

These lacquers contain very powerful solvents, and if the piece has been spirit- or oil-stained, there is the risk of the colour bleeding.

The lacquers are often in the form of a sanding sealer, making them suitable for use as a base for wax polishing as described above. They produce a very low lustre in their own right without resorting to burnishing, but burnishing will eliminate any adhering dust.

Two-pack Catalysed Lacquers

Sanding sealers are not necessary here, as the lacquer has a high build. Remember that once the catalyst has been added to the lacquer, the pot life is limited, and, above all, never put back unused lacquer into the container. Follow the instructions for mixing lacquer and catalyst to the letter, as the proportions are quite critical. The first coat can be thinned with the special thinners provided in the lacquer kit.

Large items can be brush-coated: follow the procedure described for cellulose/melamine above, but allow more time for hardening, say a couple of hours. Small items such as light pulls can be dipped, as shown in Fig 11.6, and hung up to dry; the lacquer should be thinned down a little more, as dipping leads to a heavier coating. Since the lacquer hardens by chemical action after the initial evaporation of solvent, the thicker coat should not lead to the problems of softness associated with finishes that rely entirely on solvent evaporation for hardening.

Catalysed lacquers can be burnished on the lathe at slow speed, but allow a couple of days for the catalytic action to do its job.

Fig 11.6 Dipping.

CHAPTER 12

Protecting Timber

T imber is a quite remarkable material, in that it has phenomenal durability when environmental conditions are right; but on the other hand, if the conditions are not right, wooden structures can be destroyed in a frighteningly short time. This chapter is concerned with those factors which lead to its destruction, and with how timber can best be protected.

It is an unpleasant fact of life that any naturally occurring organic material will have at least one living organism capable of using it as a food supply. Wood is no exception to this rule, which has evolved to ensure that nutrients locked up inside organic material become recycled. The main agents in this process are insects, usually the larval stage, and fungi. The two are frequently linked, in that the tunnels created by the burrowing larvae allow the entry of fungal spores. This invasion by fungi is often an independent event, but on some occasions there is an association between the fungus and the insect, which carries the spores into the wood as the larva burrows its way through.

A less obvious risk to wood is strong sunlight: long-term exposure to ultraviolet radiation results in chemical changes to the structure of wood fibres and brings about a degrading of the wood. However, fire remains the most devastating enemy. It is also the least easy to provide protection against.

INSECT ATTACK

In nature, insect infestation of wood (either in the living tree or in the dead, fallen state) is usually the first stage in the recycling process. There are many species that include part of their life cycle in wood, but as far as furniture and structural timbers are concerned we are worried by a smaller number, mostly those that can live in relatively dry conditions. However, fungal attack causes the moisture level of wood to increase, and in these conditions the wood can undergo secondary insect infestation – by weevils or woodlice, for example. These insects are unwelcome, of course, but in these circumstances they must be considered as harmless, as the only reason for their presence is the already irretrievably decayed state of the stock; they are not able to survive in healthy wood. Under this onslaught the wood can be reduced to a pile of powder, with only strands of the harder areas remaining intact (*see* Fig 12.1).

Fig 12.1 The appearance of wet rot: timber is reduced to a soggy, fibrous mass.

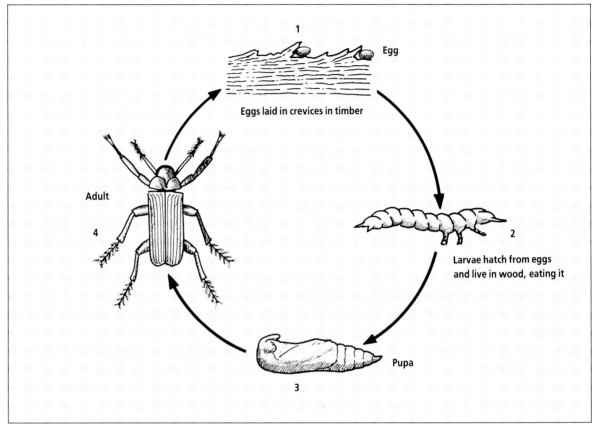

1
Egg

Eggs laid in crevices in timber

2
Larvae hatch from eggs
and live in wood, eating it

Adult
4

Pupa
3

**Fig 12.2 Life cycle of woodboring insects: the adult stage is relatively short,
while the highly destructive larval stage may last for years.**

The most obvious signs of insect infestation are the exit holes, the points where the adult insects have chewed their way to the surface of the timber before flying off. The adult stage is normally short-lived and, after mating, the female lays her eggs on the surface of the timber. After the eggs hatch, the young larvae burrow their way into the wood to begin their destructive life cycle. This part of the life cycle can last for several years, depending upon the species, during which time they chew their way through the structure, forming tunnels. 'Worm holes' are in fact the exit holes caused by the mature insect escaping. These holes are not a true indication of the extent to which the wood has been excavated and its structure weakened. Nevertheless, a large area covered with exit holes should be taken as an indication of very serious damage to the timber's structure, although this might only be localized. Fig 12.2 illustrates in general terms the life cycle of woodboring insects; species tend to differ only in the length of the different stages.

Common Furniture Beetle

This is one of the commonest of timber pests, and is or has been present in most old houses and a good deal of old furniture. The adult beetle emerges during the summer months, an event often marked by the appearance of fine wood dust (frass). The beetles only live for a couple of weeks, and mate very soon after emerging.

The female lays her eggs in crevices, on end grain or rough timber; never on smooth surfaces. When buying or inspecting old furniture, it pays,

Common Furniture Beetle

PHOTOGRAPH COURTESY OF RENTOKIL LTD.

Fig 12.3 (a) Common furniture beetle.

PHOTOGRAPH COURTESY OF RENTOKIL LTD.

Fig 12.3 (b) Exit holes of the common furniture beetle.

Deathwatch Beetle

Fig 12.4 (a) Deathwatch beetle.

PHOTOGRAPH COURTESY OF RENTOKIL LTD.

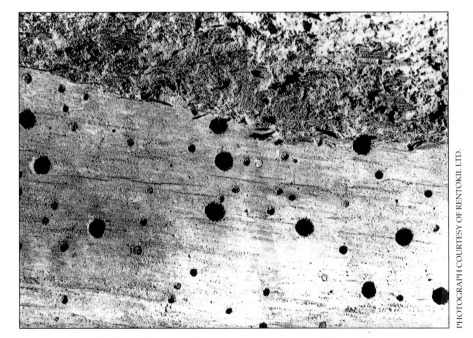

Fig 12.4 (b) Deathwatch beetle flight holes (large); the small
holes are made by the common furniture beetle.

PHOTOGRAPH COURTESY OF RENTOKIL LTD.

therefore, to inspect the backs, the inside of frames and other hidden areas, as these will be favoured by the beetle. The larval stage lasts for at least two years, depending upon the temperature, humidity and type of timber. The ideal conditions for beetles are a temperature of around 22°C and air humidity of around 50%; they therefore favour older houses without central heating.

The exit holes of the furniture beetle are about 1.5mm–2mm (¹⁄₁₆in) in diameter. Recent holes are light in colour on the inside, while older ones tend to darken with age and accumulated dirt. Frass is also associated with these. You may also see a number of very small holes (less than 1mm) situated nearby; these are caused by a group of small insects called chalcids, that prey on the furniture beetle larvae. Their larvae have the charming habit of living as parasites on the beetle larvae, killing them in the process. The adult chalcid either emerges through an old beetle exit hole or creates very small ones of its own. Fig 12.3 shows the typical exit holes of the furniture beetle and the adult insect; note the small exit holes of the chalcid beetle.

Deathwatch Beetle

This is one of the larger woodboring beetles, whose presence is almost exclusively confined to oak structural timbers. The eggs are laid in April or May, and the larvae may take 5–10 years to complete their stage of the life cycle before the adult beetles emerge. As you might expect, the exit holes are large, at 3mm–5mm (⅛in– almost ¼in) diameter (see Fig 12.4).

Long-horn Beetles

This is yet another group of species that attacks structural timbers (see Fig 12.5). Some species attack softwood, while others prefer hardwood; the larvae of the former are frequently imported into the house in bark-covered timber. The exit

holes are a characteristic oval shape. Some species, such as the house long-horn, are very damaging to structural timbers; fortunately, the house long-horn is not very common in this country, and the other species are only a real problem in timbers retaining their bark. Easy control is achieved by not introducing bark-covered timber into the house.

There are many other insects that will attack timber but, as already mentioned, they may be an indication of a more serious problem of dampness and fungal attack. It has already been stated that the whole process of attack by insects is a natural one, and it is frequently possible to transfer the creatures when bringing timber indoors. Any felled timber that has spent a good deal of time lying around, especially if it has seen a spring and summer in that state, should always be treated with suspicion. It pays to remove the bark and sapwood beforehand, as these are the vulnerable parts of the timber.

Other preventive measures include the maintenance of a dry environment. Centrally heated houses are, somewhat paradoxically, a fairly hostile sort of environment: while the temperature may be ideal, central heating usually brings a reduction in the air humidity levels, and reduced wood moisture levels with it.

While prevention is always better than cure, it is not always successful, and so we need to rely on eradication. The brief descriptions of life cycles given above would seem to indicate that the spring and summer months are quite crucial to the insects, as during this time the adults mate and the female lays her eggs. These, then, are the months when you should be vigilant in looking out for the telltale signs. Examine all surfaces of the wood, especially the normally unseen areas, such as the backs of cabinets, for new holes. If you find an area where the holes look particularly light in colour or there is fresh frass around, assume an attack.

Large-scale attacks to structural timbers by furniture beetles or attacks by deathwatch or

Long-horn Beetle

Fig 12.5 (a) Long-horn beetle.

Fig 12.5 (b) Long-horn beetle flight holes.

house long-horn beetles should be dealt with by one of the pest control organizations. The chemicals required to eradicate pests are poisons, and a large-scale operation needs very close supervision of the way in which they are used, so refer the problem to a specialist company. Small-scale attacks, such as those associated with furniture, are quite easy to deal with.

The aim of pest control is to prevent reinfestation and to destroy any larvae that are still in the wood. The holes appear because an insect has burrowed its way out, not the other way around, so it may appear that we are bolting the stable door after the event, but there are other considerations. For example, there may be larvae present in the wood at a different stage of their life cycle, and treatment will, we hope, kill them. Treatment of nearby furniture is a good idea, because of the obvious danger of cross-infestation.

Treatment

There are a number of proprietary woodworm treatment products, and there is not much to choose between them in terms of efficiency, as they are all strong insecticides.

The vulnerable areas to be treated, as already indicated, are those that are not normally visible – the backs, the inside of the tops of legs, and tops and bottoms of carcasses. Show wood is rarely the source of the problem, but may exhibit the effects with unsightly exit holes. Unpolished wood should be treated by brushing the fluid on to it and letting it soak into the surface. It is not a good idea to do this over polished show wood for two reasons:

▌ Eggs are not normally laid in these areas, so it is a waste of effort. The poisonous residue on the surface can then become a source of danger to children and pets.

▌ The residue left after the solvent has evaporated dulls the polished surface.

The best way to treat woodworm is to inject the fluid into the flight holes: this achieves greater penetration of the wood, and also makes it more difficult for any remaining larvae to spread or for new larvae to enter via the old exit holes. On a relatively small item of furniture where the area affected is fairly small, this presents no problem; woodworm killer containers often come with a spout that acts as an injector, and this can be pushed into the holes and the can then squeezed to force the fluid in (*see* Fig 12.6). It is not necessary to inject every hole, as they frequently interconnect: inject one hole for every square inch, but be careful, as you will discover how they join up when, during the process of injecting one hole, the fluid squirts out of another.

Any other furniture in the room should be given some protection by painting solution on to the areas of wood not in sight, as explained before. This will help to reduce cross-infestation.

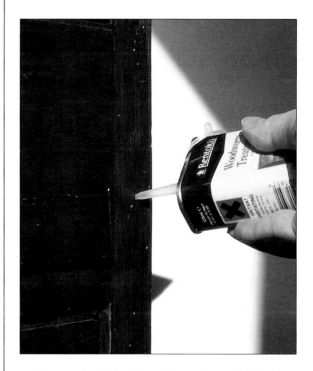

Fig 12.6 Inject flight holes with woodworm fluid, using an inexpensive applicator which can be bought separately. The smaller tins of fluid have an injector incorporated into the top.

Because these substances are toxic, it is necessary to observe the simple rules of hygiene after using them: wash your hands, and try to limit contact with the skin; do not attempt to spray the liquid. There will be an odour after the treatment, but this will disappear after a day.

In addition to the woodworm fluids, there are special anti-woodworm wax polishes containing the insecticide, and it is worthwhile dressing all show wood with this, especially where such wood exhibits flight holes.

Finally, because of the extended life cycle of the larvae, it will be necessary to keep an eye on the items for a couple of years, to ensure successful elimination has occurred. It is worth repeating the process of painting woodworm fluid on to unseen timbers during the spring following the initial treatment.

FUNGAL ATTACK

While fungi are, in biological terms, among the most important living organisms on the planet, as they are responsible for decomposing organic matter and thereby releasing materials for re-cycling, they are not particularly welcome when their action causes timber to disintegrate before our eyes! The problem may be compounded by the fact that the softening effect on the wood fibres then encourages animal pests to invade.

Fungi propagate by spores which are dispersed in the air. These spores can lie dormant for very long periods before springing to life again when conditions for fungal growth are right. The most important condition is that of timber moisture: most fungi that attack timber prefer a moisture level of around 30%–50%. The vulnerable timbers are all exterior constructions, timbers in contact with the soil or any ground outside, or where interior conditions give rise to high levels of moisture – perhaps through poor ventilation, especially after the wood has received a soaking, such as following a flooding. Providing recently soaked wood is dried out fairly quickly, there is little danger of serious fungal damage as a result of a single event; however, repeated or extended periods of high moisture levels will eventually

Fig 12.7 If wet rot is not dealt with early, large-scale destruction is inevitable: the disintegrated, fibrous mass to which the timber becomes reduced will lead to secondary infestation by invertebrates such as wood lice.

PHOTOGRAPH COURTESY OF RENTOKIL LTD.

Fig 12.8 (a) The characteristic appearance of dry rot.

lead to wood rot, unless adequate protection has been afforded.

The first sign of fungal attack often takes the form of patches of blue-black discolouration caused by mildew-type fungi; the spectacular discolourations in so-called 'spalted' timber (and also 'brown oak') are caused in this way. These fungal attacks are not in themselves particularly damaging, but should be taken as a sign that, if left unchecked, the wood will deteriorate as fungi take over.

The damage is caused by the way fungi feed; this is a process called external digestion, where the filament-like fibres of the fungus produce digestive juices that are sent into the wood. The wood fibres are literally digested outside the fungus, and the nutrients then absorbed into the fungus. The wood becomes soft and spongy and its moisture level rises, making the conditions for further deterioration ideal, so the process is almost self-perpetuating. Finally, the structure of the timber is destroyed and it crumbles away as a soggy, fibrous mess. Fig 12.7 is a typical example of the damage caused by wet rot, as this process is known.

In extreme cases it will be necessary to cut away the affected timber and replace it with new, sound wood. That said, the progress of wet rot is relatively slow when compared with the rampant spread of dry rot, which is normally associated with timbers that appear to be completely dry, or very nearly so.

In fact, the fungus that causes dry rot, *Merulius lacrymans*, will thrive in timber with a moisture level as low as 20%. The problem is that once the fungus has established itself it can spread to dry timbers (hence the name), because it can survive on the moisture gained from the original damp timber. The fungus can spread very rapidly in two ways: first, it will generate millions of spores that become distributed through the air; second, it can spread by sending out from the main body many fibres, called hyphae, which seek out new sources of nourishment – i.e. timber – and may even pass over several metres of masonry and cement in its search, even though these provide no nourishment whatsoever. The main body of the fungus will supply these hyphae with nourishment until new timber has been located, and it begins to digest that too. The consequence of this is that, while wet rot is relatively slow to spread, dry rot can be rampant and spread with frightening speed (*see* Fig 12.8).

A dry rot infection is best dealt with by a professional builder or a company that specializes in pest eradication. The treatment usually involves a radical removal of timber adjacent to the attack, because you can never be too sure of how far the hyphae or spores have reached. The liberal application of fungicides, both on the remaining timber and the new replacement timber, ensures that eradication has been completed.

PHOTOGRAPH COURTESY OF RENTOKIL LTD.

Fig 12.8 (b) Dry rot damage.

Treatment

The affected areas need to be cut away and replaced with new, sound timber. It is important that **all** affected wood is removed, as any fungus left behind will become the source of further destruction. This means that you will need to cut back to well beyond the obvious area of infection and will need to remove some good, sound timber as well.

Finally, the timber will need a coat of preservative, to provide protection against future attack. As always, prevention is better than cure in these matters: bearing in mind that fungi generally attack damp timber, it is obvious that the best preventive measure is to ensure that timbers remain dry – either by eliminating sources of moisture or by ensuring that vulnerable timbers are given adequate ventilation, such as roof spaces in buildings open directly to the outside. Timber thus treated will rarely be attacked, but regular inspection is advisable. Furniture is rarely attacked by fungi, as the moisture level in the timber in even the worst domestic environments is unlikely to reach a vulnerable state.

Timbers which are likely to be constantly wet and exposed to moisture will need preventive treatment. The usual method takes the form of an annual ritual (chore?) of preservative application.

PRESERVATIVES

All wood preservatives are poisons: their intention is to kill off wood-attacking insects and fungi. Many of the newer formulations make the claim of being harmless to plants and pets, and this is certainly true once the stuff has dried, but during use they are still very unpleasant substances.

The choice of which preservative to use depends on a number of factors, but some questions should be answered before making your choice, as a 'horses for courses' rule again applies here. Manufacturers tend to formulate their products for specific purposes. The questions you should answer – and then match up your requirements to the qualities and function of the product – are:

▌ Is it for internal or external use?

▌ Will I be painting the wood or finishing it in some other way after the preservative has been applied?

▌ What decorative properties do I require? In other words, am I applying this to a garden fence which is made of rough timber, or to a new front door to my house, which must have a high quality and resilient finish?

There is a confusing array of choice. A trip to the local DIY superstore will confirm the problem, in that the shelves are filled with preservatives specially designed for one or another purpose. By answering the three questions set out above, you can narrow down the choice to a few products appropriate to the circumstances.

Constructional Timbers

The oldest and cheapest of these preservatives is creosote. This is a coal tar product which, while effective, is toxic to plants, wildlife and pets – not to mention unpleasant to work with and smelly!

Modern preparations are based on synthetic chemicals, and there is a general tendency towards meeting the market demand for 'safe' products: once dried, the product is safe for plants and animals to come into contact with it. While most of these preparations are solvent-based, there are a number of water-based ones, which have a number of attractions, not least the lack of odour. However, water-based preservatives are only suitable for rough-sawn timber such as fencing, and are often marketed as suitable for garden timbers.

Timbers in contact with the ground or exposed to extreme weather need the deeper penetrating preservatives designed for these conditions. They are usually formulated to give extra protection against fungal decay, because the timbers they are designed to protect are likely to be wet for very extended periods; it is possible that they may never be dry.

Almost all of these products are strongly pigmented, to provide additional protection from the sun's ultraviolet radiation, which is damaging both to the wood and the preservative itself. UV is an effective decomposer of organic material – the high-energy rays actually break down chemical bonds – so special UV-absorbing

Fig 12.9 An exterior door treated with a 'woodstain' product; note the cloudy appearance of the timber, caused by the opacity of the pigments in the varnish.

pigments are present in the preservative to reduce this effect.

Colourless preservatives are also available, but should not be used on their own for exterior timbers, because of the problem with UV; they are, however, perfectly all right to use with internal timbers. There are many situations where it is desirable to use a preservative that does not change the colour of the wood: for example, you may wish to protect wooden floors and yet retain the natural colour, or want to paint or varnish vulnerable timbers such as exterior doors or window frames.

You will frequently come across wooden structures, particularly in horticultural or agricultural settings, with a green tinge to them. They have been treated with a preservative formulated with a green colour, which is often used in circumstances where the natural green is a pleasant alternative to darker varieties. It is a general purpose preservative, and the colour makes it possible to identify treated areas.

Show Wood

A preservative is of little value if it does not penetrate the surface of the wood, and the deeper the penetration, the greater the protection; if the surface also resists water penetration, then all the better. Many of the preservatives described above do offer some protection from this, thanks to the waxes and oils used in their formulation, but they may not provide the decorative properties of varnishes. In the past, yacht varnish would have been used to decorate exterior timbers (*see* Chapter 8); this has limited durability, although it will provide some protection from UV radiation and has great plasticity (flexibility).

'Woodstain' is a range of decorative products designed to provide the properties of a physical barrier, protection from UV and some limited protection from fungal attack. They are pigmented moisture-permeable varnishes (*see* Chapter 8),

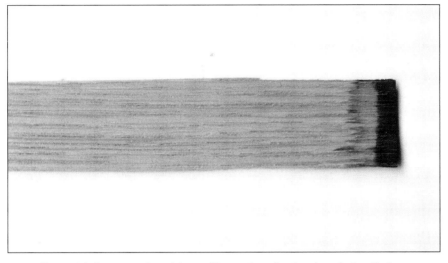

Fig 12.10 A demonstration of the capillary action of end grain, a feature that can be taken advantage of when treating particularly vulnerable timbers with preservative.

and the latest generation of these varnishes is water-based (acrylic), which are obviously more convenient to use.

Now, since protection can only be provided to that portion of the wood containing the preservative, these materials are probably not as effective as preservatives (except against surface mildew and algae), especially if the varnish coat becomes damaged, allowing both moisture and fungal spores to penetrate. The best protection is provided by treating the wood with a colourless preservative prior to using the wood stain varnish; major joinery manufacturers frequently apply preservatives to their exterior products in the factory.

Fig 12.9 shows a door treated with a modern 'woodstain' product. No more than two or three coats should usually be applied, or they will become less permeable to internal moisture. Properly applied, such varnishes will last for up to six years with conscientious maintenance (*see* Chapter 8). There is one negative feature of these products, in that the pigments used frequently lead to a slight opacity, especially as far as the darker tones are concerned. The result of this can be that the natural figuring of the timber is sometimes partially obliterated.

DRAWBACKS

Slapping on a coat or two of preservative does not automatically provide 100% protection: the chemical will only penetrate a few millimetres into the timber, so the internal structure remains vulnerable. It is possible to increase the protection by applying preservative under pressure, but this can only be done under factory conditions. End grain is particularly vulnerable, and such areas need to be well soaked. If time and facilities permit, the ends of posts that will be embedded in the ground should be left soaking in preservative overnight, to allow the natural capillary action draw the liquid right up into the wood (*see* Fig 12.10). However, the practice of using metal bases to posts means that this particular expense will almost certainly defray the deferred costs of replacing fence posts later on.

Anything which damages the surface and creates a break in the protective layer will, in time, lead to the timber becoming attacked from within, as fungi can penetrate and work on the wet internal structure. Therefore, any pretreated timber which is cut must have the exposed unprotected surfaces treated.

CHAPTER 13

A Guide to Refinishing

FURNITURE

K nowing when and how to refinish furniture is often regarded as a problem area; common sense and care will go a long way to solving the problems.

PATINA

The importance of patination cannot be ignored when dealing with restoration work, as it is an indicator of age and, by implication, of authenticity. Absence of it makes collectors suspicious and reduces the value of the item in the saleroom. However, a line must be drawn between genuine patina – the mellowing of a surface through use, generations of hand polishing and exposure to light – and grime or real damage.

Patina is a property of the polish film and wood surface: a part of the furniture, not something on the surface that can be removed by cleaning. For example, it is generally accepted that minor dents and scratches are legitimate forms of patination, since they are not really disfiguring, but a cigarette burn is damage, which it is permissible to repair. Stripping old polished surfaces and staining and repolishing, even using traditional methods and materials, will destroy valuable patina and must only be carried out under extreme circumstances – and only then by someone competent to do so in such a way that will retain or restore as much patina as possible.

In many instances, a good restorer can reproduce the patina if, for one reason or another, stripping cannot be avoided. This is a highly skilled technique, demanding a thorough knowledge of how things *should* look; after a restoration, the workpiece should ideally look as though it had never been touched. The bottom line is: wherever possible, avoid stripping an old surface; there are usually better alternatives, especially if the old surface is basically sound.

CRITERIA FOR STRIPPING

Start from the premise that stripping is unnecessary and undesirable unless:

▌The old finish is badly damaged, i.e. flaking off or very badly worn.

▌The new finish is not compatible with the old, i.e. a French polish cannot be put over an ordinary varnish, because it will peel off through lack of adhesion.

▌The old finish is known to be a modern lacquer, i.e. it cannot be repaired because a good bond between old and new finishes will not be obtained (this does not apply to polyurethane varnishes, which can be repaired successfully if not too far gone).

▌The colour of the wood has been badly faded by strong sunlight and needs to be restored.

Under no circumstances should an old, and possibly valuable piece of furniture be stripped by anyone other than a professional restorer. Other items can be refinished by the amateur without losing value, but even here it is not always necessary to strip; if the old finish is basically sound, it can be improved.

IDENTIFYING FINISHES

Apart from nitrocellulose, modern finishes are difficult to positively identify as a particular type, as they will not soften if subjected to rubbing with a cloth moistened with solvents. They are non-reversible, and this fact alone can be used as a means of positive identification, because you will know that it must be a precatalysed or acid-catalysed cellulose, two-part polyurethane, polyester, etc.

Before testing to determine the nature of the material, you can more or less infer what the finish is likely to be by the age of the object: anything over 50 years old is likely to be finished in a spirit-based varnish or French polish, post-war furniture will very likely be finished in an early nitrocellulose, and contemporary furniture will be finished in one of the catalysed lacquers.

It is difficult to be absolutely certain about such things, because an old piece may have been refinished fairly recently, in which case the finish is likely to be a cellulose-based lacquer (if refinished professionally) or polyurethane varnish (if finished by an amateur). The latter will probably be characterized by brushmarks, possibly with dust specks and small fragments of bristle.

In other words, the nature of the finish will be discovered partly by testing, partly by knowledge of an item's age and partly by knowledge of the piece's history. If you do not know what finish has been applied, Table 5 explains how to test with solvents to arrive at an answer.

The table works by a process of elimination, asking questions and guiding you to others: start at 1, and if the answer is that the finish will not soften with meths, you are told to move to 2, and so on, until you arrive at a final answer. When testing a surface with solvents or by scraping, choose a small and inconspicuous area. The solvent should be applied with a soft clean cloth, but begin by cleaning that area with soap and water, to remove grime that could confuse the result of the test.

TABLE 5

1	Finish softened with meths	FRENCH POLISH OR SPIRIT VARNISH
	Not softened with meths	GO TO 2
2	Finish softened with white spirit	GO TO 3
	Finish not softened with white spirit	GO TO 4
3	Finish feels waxy and smears when rubbed with a finger; will scrape off when scratched with fingernail	WAX
	Surface feels oily smooth, but will not smear or scrape off with fingernail	OIL
4	If scraped with blade of sharp knife, finish will produce tiny flakes with some dust	POLYURETHANE VARNISH
	If scraped with blade of sharp knife, forms a white dust	GO TO 5
5	Will soften with cellulose thinners	CELLULOSE LACQUER
	Will not soften with cellulose thinners	CATALYSED LACQUER

WAX AND OIL FINISHES

These are easily 'repaired': marks caused by heat, moisture and handling are removed by wiping over the surface with white spirit or pure turpentine, allowed to dry again and then recoated with wax polish or furniture oil.

FRENCH POLISH

A neglected polished surface will be dull with accumulated dirt and old wax: if it has been regularly polished with an aerosol polish or with wax pastes over a long period of time, the surface can become very greasy and dull. Such a surface will benefit from the use of a reviver.

First, clean the surface with a solution of one teaspoon of washing soda in a pint (0.56l) of warm water, using a well wrung-out chamois leather. Allow to dry, and then test for any remaining deposits of wax by rubbing the surface with a fingernail: if it is still dirty, greasy deposits will lift off. Wash again until all dirt has been removed. After drying there will still be a dullness, and possibly some whitish streaks, due to residue. These can be removed with a reviver; recipes can be found in Chapter 16.

Apply the reviver sparingly with a pad of stockinette, working a small area at a time with circular movements. As the area brightens, change to straight strokes and finish off by buffing with a clean piece of stockinette. Revive the whole surface in this way before finally buffing it all with a clean pad.

If, after all this, the French polish is still dull, or even shows signs of wear, it will need to be repolished to bring back the shine. It will not be necessary to strip, but the old polish should be prepared first by cutting back with 600 grit wet-or-dry paper, used wet (a little detergent in the water acts as a wetting agent and makes the task easier) – *see* Fig 13.3. The aim is to create a uniform dullness over the whole surface and to thus key it in preparation for rebodying. Once the surface has been cut back in this way, rebody with French polish thinned a little (one part of meths to three of polish), and finish by stiffing. (Chapter 7 gives instructions on French polishing.)

Of course, all this assumes that the French polish is without serious blemishes. There may be marks and other defects that require special treatment.

Ring Marks or Cloudy Areas

White marks are caused by water or heat, and can be easily removed or, at least, reduced. Mix some cigarette ash to a paste with raw linseed oil, and apply the paste with a finger wrapped in a cloth. Apply a fair amount of pressure, and rub along the grain over the ring (*see* Fig 13.1). Faint blemishes will begin to respond quite quickly, while heavier areas may need two or more applications over a period of a few days. Wipe off any surplus oil afterwards, and clean the whole surface with a reviver. The marks may not disappear altogether, but they will look much less obvious.

Dark rings occur if very hot dishes are allowed to rest on the surface, and the heat has discoloured the wood beneath. Scorch marks can only be treated in the same way as cigarette burns, i.e. by stripping off the polish and scraping the scorched fibres. Dark marks are also caused by water penetrating the polish and discolouring the wood; the only cure is to strip the old polish and bleach out the stain with oxalic acid or 20 vol. hydrogen peroxide (*see* Chapter 5 for information on mixing and using these bleaches; but remember that both oxalic acid and hydrogen peroxide are dangerous substances, and should be used in accordance with the health and safety information on the packaging), then restain and polish as required. This action is drastic, however, and careful consideration

Removing Ring Marks

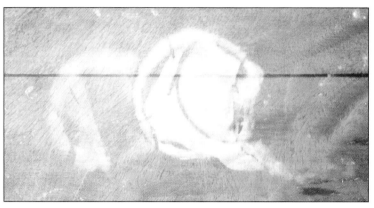

1 Fig 13.1 (a) Before. A fair amount of pressure applied with a finger along the grain will be needed to remove white ring marks and cloudy areas caused by water.

2 Fig 13.1 (b) During application.

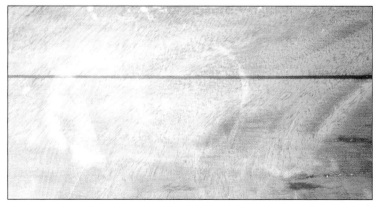

3 Fig 13.1 (c) After. It may take several attempts with the linseed oil to remove the ring altogether.

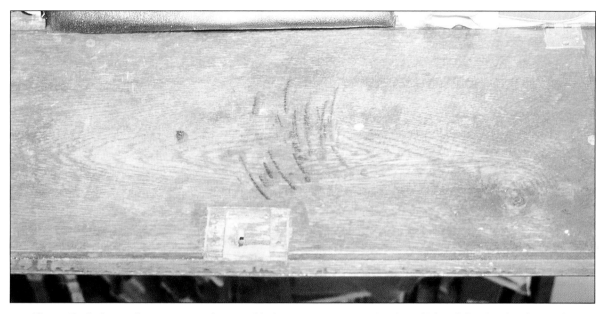

Fig 13.2 Dark ring marks or spots may be caused by heat or water penetrating the polish and discolouring the wood
beneath. Some ring marks are the result of ink, but the difference is usually fairly obvious.

should be given to it: if you can live with the marks, do so rather than risking ruining a good piece of furniture.

Desks and bureaux are often found with small black (or red or blue) rings caused by ink (*see* Fig 13.2). Here there is often little to be done, other than trying to live with the blemish. Under no circumstances attempt to strip a valuable piece. In the case of ink stains, a little weak oxalic acid can be applied to the ring, to see if it can be bleached. Do not leave it on the area for too long, or it will produce its own mark: if it is going to work, it will do so quite quickly. Clean off the acid afterwards with a little warm water and detergent, and buff dry.

Other ring marks show up as areas of polish that have been removed completely; this blemish is usually caused by alcohol on the bottoms of glasses – *see* Chapter 10.

Scratches

Very minor scratches can be darkened by rubbing over with a little raw linseed oil and wiping off the surplus. If the scratch is very white, due to

the wood beneath also being scratched, mix in a little powder pigment of an appropriate colour. Major scratches may necessitate stripping and repolishing.

If you have a steady hand, the scratch can be painted out by mixing a little pigment in some thinned French polish (one part of meths to three of polish); carefully apply this to the scratch with a pencil brush, having first cleaned up the whole surface. Once the applied polish has dried, repolish the surface to disguise the blemish. You must take care in touching up, or it will show up as an obvious ridge or smudge. (Chapter 10 gives more information on colouring.)

Flaking or Crazed Polish

There is not a lot you can do here other than strip and repolish, as the old finish is in the process of disintegration.

Burns

These have to be ignored, touched up with pigmented polish as described in Chapter 10, or given a professional repair.

POLYURETHANE VARNISH AND
SYNTHETIC LACQUERS

Repairs to such surfaces are generally limited; you may be able to treat white heat and water marks or disguise minor scratches as described above, but the only sure method is to strip and repolish.

Polyurethane can be rubbed down with fine wet-or-dry abrasive paper to try and remove a blemish, and given a new coat of varnish afterwards. In any event, if you intend to recoat polyurethane, always provide a key by using wet-or-dry in this way. A synthetic lacquered surface is not so easy to repair, and you may well find that the only action to take will be to strip it down and repolish.

JOINERY

In considering joinery, painted surfaces are not within the scope of this book.

POLYURETHANE AND
YACHT VARNISHES

If the varnish film is mostly sound, with perhaps a little flaking and some bare patches, the surface should be washed down (avoiding bare areas), allowed to dry, rubbed down with 240 grit abrasive and recoated with one or two coats of varnish after wiping with a tack rag (follow the procedure for smoothing down between coats as outlined in Chapter 8).

Where varnish stains are being used and the surface has bare areas, even small ones, you may need to strip completely and treat the surface as a new surface for revarnishing; if you do not, the areas that were bare may show up darker.

Peeling varnish is an indication of progressive loss of adhesion, and it is wise to strip and revarnish.

MICROPOROUS VARNISHES

These are treated in exactly the same way as polyurethane, except that only one coat of new varnish is applied. The important thing to remember is that a microporous varnish cannot be used over a non-MPV varnish, such as polyurethane or yacht varnish, because its permeability will be lost: it is essential to strip off these other varnishes first.

PRESERVATIVES

These tend to weather and fade naturally (if coloured), and, provided they are not a varnish-based compound, can simply be recoated. If you want to use one of the new generation of water-based compounds on wood that was originally coated with solvent-based material, such as creosote, you must make sure that the old material is well weathered. Depending upon the conditions, recoating should take place every couple of years to ensure maximum protection.

STRIPPING

Adequate descriptions of the use of proprietary paint and varnish strippers are given on the side of the cans. However, there are a number of points, and a few hints, that should be mentioned for good results to be obtained.

PREPARING FOR STRIPPING

Proprietary strippers are based on a powerful solvent, methylene chloride, and alcohol. This means they evaporate, and the fumes can be dangerous in confined spaces: very good ventilation is essential, and if you have chronic respiratory problems, or are sensitive to fumes, use a respirator. Put down lots of newspaper on the floor beneath the work, adding enough for an area for splashes (*see* Fig 13.3). Have an old bucket filled with cold water to hand, so that as the softened varnish is lifted off the wood, it is dropped into the bucket, out of harm's way.

Protective clothing should include heavy-duty rubber gloves of industrial quality – household gloves will dissolve!

Fig 13.3 also shows an item of furniture ready for stripping. Note that it has been dismantled as far as it is practicable to do so; this means that the doors have been taken off and the drawers pulled out. Door and drawer furniture, including hinges, is removed to reduce obstructions. Each dismantled 'bit' effectively becomes another separate item to strip, so the whole work can be sectioned off into manageable areas.

Do not use shavehook scrapers when removing the softened polish, as they have a tendency to dig into the wood; modify an old cabinet scraper or wallpaper scraper, as shown in Fig 13.4. 00 grade wire wool can be used to remove material from awkward places such as carvings and mouldings – a scraper will simply dig in and damage the wood.

The first coat of stripper should be brushed on like paint; this provides a key by roughening the surface. After a couple of minutes, apply a very generous second coat; leave this for at least 10 minutes on varnished surfaces. Don't be mean with it, either: it is expensive stuff, but skimping will only result in having to spend more time and use more stripper. There should be a very substantial layer of stripper on the surface, but not so much that it runs all over the place. Work the stuff well into crevices and corners with a stabbing action of the brush.

Fig 13.3 Preparations for stripping: plenty of newspapers protect the floor, and the piece to be stripped is dismantled as far as possible.

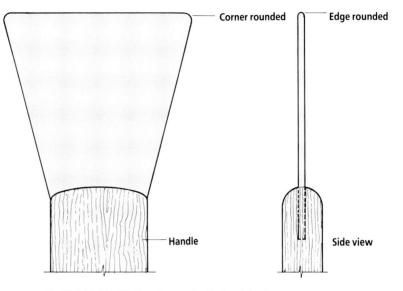

Fig 13.4 (a) Modified wallpaper knife for stripping.

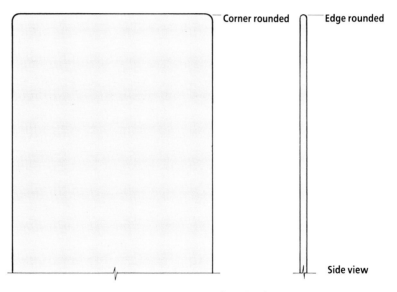

Fig 13.4 (b) Modified cabinet scraper for stripping.

As for the different brands of stripper, they are very much the same, but always look for the magic phrases 'non-caustic' or 'non-acid'; this means they will be kind to the wood. Always neutralize stripped surfaces afterwards, even if the material is described as self-neutralizing. I always use meths (even with strippers that describe themselves as being neutralized with water) for two reasons: first, there is no grain raising, so the wood does not go 'fuzzy'; second,

the work dries much faster, and this usually means that I can strip and stain in a single day. Neutralizing with water or white spirit results in a long drying period – especially in cold weather! Never try to refinish if the work has not dried out thoroughly; it will only lead to problems.

Sometimes a finish will resist the action of strippers, even to the point where they have no effect whatsoever. This occurs with some of the catalysed lacquers, and there is little you can do about it; stripping with abrasives is one possibility, but this is laborious and is only feasible on flat surfaces. You may have to resort to commercial stripping companies.

I am frequently asked about commercial stripping and the effect of dipping tanks. There are terrible – and often true – horror stories about furniture falling apart and wood darkening or splitting, but it is not fair to generalize. **Under no circumstances** send mahogany, walnut or oak furniture to be dipped if the tanks use a caustic solution, as the wood may become badly discoloured. In addition, prolonged immersion in these caustic solutions frequently results in efflorescence later as the wood dries out at home: this is the appearance of a white powdery deposit on the surface, indicating inadequate neutralization of the caustic, and it may reappear, even if cleaned off. If this occurs, wipe over the wood with a generous helping of white malt vinegar in warm water. Allow to dry, but leave for quite a few weeks before risking refinishing.

There is now a growing number of stripping firms that specialize in non-caustic dipping; the stripper is solvent-based, and much safer for your furniture and joinery. My own experience of non-caustic dipping is that the results are much more satisfactory: water is still used at the end of the process to neutralize residue, but there is no extended immersion. There is no discoloration, and joints which were sound on entering the dipping tank remain so. However, some problems can be experienced with veneered work, as even small cracks or bubbles can result in lifting.

TREATMENT AFTER STRIPPING

After stripping, the wood is treated as if it were a new surface, and can be smoothed with abrasives, stained and repolished. You may experience a little fuzziness on the surface if water has been used to neutralize the stripper, but in general, because the surface had already been smoothed when originally polished, very little preparation is needed. Use only a fine abrasive (240 or 320 grit).

Veneers present a tricky problem in that they are very thin, and extra care needs to be exercised: use a 320 grit abrasive, and work cautiously to remove only raised fibres, not the veneer itself.

If you find that a stain will not take properly, this is very likely due to incomplete stripping. The stain simply lies on top of the wood – when wiped over, it is merely taken off again – or causes patchiness where it is absorbed in some areas but not in others. The only solution to this problem is to use the stripper again, and to rub over the work with 000 steel wool after about 10 minutes. The stripper is again neutralized as already described (*see* Fig 13.5).

Fig 13.5 The light area shows where a stain has not taken, due to the surface not being completely stripped.

Painted Finishes

aint as a decorative finish has an extremely long provenance, stretching well back into prehistory. While decorative painting of wood has been with us all the time, there are periods in our history which are associated with particular fashions and techniques; perhaps the most notable time is the eighteenth century and the Classical revival that took place under the influence of Robert Adam and others.

The very idea of painting wood is anathema to many people who believe that wood, being a natural material, ought to speak for itself. While this purist point of view cannot really be argued against, I do believe that there are many items where the quality of the construction and materials defy sympathetic treatment using stains and polishes, but where paint used creatively can regenerate an exhausted piece.

During the course of this chapter, the basic techniques of painting wood will be described. It is, however, an area of woodfinishing that cries out for an imaginative approach to the creation of an unlimited repertoire of effects. While there are some basic rules, there are few boundaries; even those rules that exist may be broken to gain an effect. For example, it is common knowledge that oil-based and water-based paints do not mix. A few years ago I painted a panel, using a mixture of white emulsion to which I added some green oil-based paint. The mixture was regularly stirred to emulsify it during the painting, and the final effect was a grainy, brushy surface. All things may not be possible, but they are worth a try!

'Junk' furniture is an ideal candidate for this form of finishing; quite often it may be the only reasonable thing to do, because the surfaces may be such an awful colour after stripping off old, treacly varnishes or paint, that even bleaching will not improve the condition.

Because furniture tends to be made up of a number of very awkward to paint components, it is better to take the piece apart and work out how best to hold or support the components while you work – a matter of lateral thinking, sometimes!

BASIC TOOLS AND MATERIALS

Detailed information on the materials and tools required for different effects will be described as they arise, but it is worth pausing to discuss the basics.

Paintbrushes

As always, if you wish to create quality, it is advisable to use tools that reflect this; in other words, buy the very best that you can afford. There are very sound practical reasons for this, and it is not simply a question of pandering to some basic ego or showmanship. A good paintbrush holds more paint and allows you to produce a better finish more easily. Not only that, it will behave itself, too – no unruly bristles poking in all directions, and certainly none that suffer from alopecia! There is nothing more frustrating or annoying than a brush that insists on shedding its bristles as you work: you cannot create a good finish this way and you will almost certainly overlook one or two bristles as you search for the offending items in the wet paint, so they will dry into the finish and spoil it.

The way a good brush is made creates a bristle profile that lends itself to feathering in. Cheap brushes have their bristles chopped across, giving a square profile (this encourages them to 'fly away'), and they have fewer bristles. Good brushes have a domed cross section, and each bristle is actually split at the end, creating finer bristle tips for laying on the paint. Figs 14.1 (a) and (b) show the anatomies of good and bad paintbrushes.

You may need different types of brush to use to create particular effects; these are described later. You will need a range of widths, as you would with any paint job.

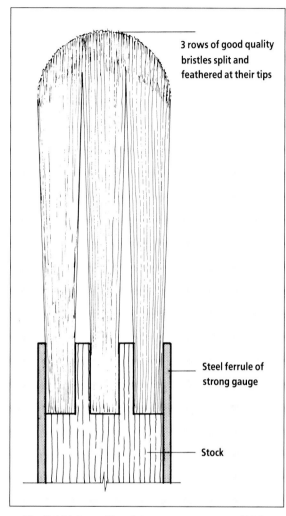

Fig 14.1 (a) A good brush has a generous crop of high quality tapered bristles set in the whole of the stock.

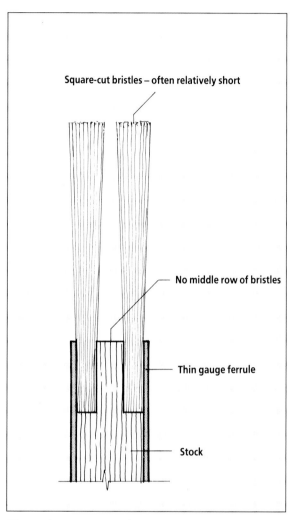

Fig 14.1 (b) A bad brush often has short, square-cut bristles, with none set into the centre of the stock.

Another point to bear in mind is that many of the finishes described in this chapter will need to be given a protective coat or two of varnish. As already explained in Chapter 8, you must reserve brushes specifically and exclusively for this task.

Artists' brushes are an essential investment for many finishes, and a range of sizes will be needed to meet specific purposes. Sable brushes would be ideal, because of their soft but controllable nature, but nylon or a similar synthetic material are a good alternative. The stiffer bristles such as hoghair are unsuitable, as they will not produce a fine finish.

Paint

Gloss paint is not part of this list, as it does not lend itself to the sort of techniques described here, not does it look all that good. As mentioned in Chapter 4, any blemishes in the wood tend to be exacerbated by the finish that goes over them. The higher the sheen, the worse the blemish looks. What follows is a list of paint types that are used:

Wood priming paint Either traditional solvent-based or, better still, the more recent water-based products. These newer products are acrylic-based, and have the advantage of being fast-drying.

Eggshell/satin finish The very low sheen of these paints makes them ideal for a number of reasons. They do not exactly mask blemishes, but they certainly do not make them as obvious as full gloss paint does. Another important feature is that they tend to be much smoother, too, with fewer brushmarks showing through. This is quite important because these paints often form the base upon which other paints are overlaid. The property required here is the ability to let glazes, for example, be spread over the paint's surface and then manipulated to create various effects, such as marbling.

Either solvent- or water-based products may be used. Acrylic eggshell/satin finish is available, although it is possible, at a pinch, to use vinyl silk, but I find the gloss of the vinyl product just a little too high. There is one word of warning here concerning the use of water-based paints: they do not yet have the flow characteristics of their solvent-based relatives, so greater care needs to be exercised to prevent brushmarks.

One very important point here is the quality of paint to be used: this can be crucial, as the cheaper brands do not lend themselves to the properties we look for. The best materials for our purpose are professional quality trade paints.

Artists' colours These can be oil- or water-based, depending on what is required for the job in hand. In general, on the basis that oil and water do not mix, whenever any effect is created using water-based paints, then water-based artists' colour will also be used.

The oil colours may be mixed with oil-based white eggshell to tint it, or may be made up into a transparent glaze, to be painted over the eggshell and then manipulated into various effects.

Water-based colours come in a variety of mediums, but the best from the point of view of economy and drying characteristics are the acrylics. Designers' gouache provides a more intense colour, and is economical when used to tint water-based paints.

You will frequently need to mix colours together to produce another colour: in order to do this successfully, you can only mix those with a similar medium. Water-based paints will mix with other water-based products, and in the same way, oil-based paints are mixed with other oil-based products.

Synthetic lacquers Chapter 9 covers synthetic lacquers in detail; they are available as solid colours very much like paint. Since they are sprayed on to the work, again refer to Chapter 9 for equipment and methods.

Glazes and Washes

For many painted effects, the colour is applied as a thin glaze or wash, which are transparent colours produced by thinning artists' colours with the appropriate solvent.

Glazes There are many effects where layers of colour need to be manipulated over a base coat. Oil colours are much slower-drying than water-colour, so by taking some artists' oil colour and thinning it to a liquid with either pure turpentine or white spirit, you have created a glaze. The definition of a glaze, then, is thinned oil colour or paint, and the result is a transparent colour that is fluid and can be manipulated, as in marbling.

Some thought and planning will need to be done when using a glaze; even though it is slow-drying, it loses some of its ability to be manipulated once the solvent has evaporated ('flashed' off), and so you should not cover at any one time an area larger than can be tackled within 20 minutes. This may not seem long, but it is longer than you would have with water-based and all other oil-bound paints.

The simple glaze described above is frequently used by artists to create such effects as skies in a landscape. The problem from our point of view is that this recipe produces a glaze that is more difficult to manipulate, and which also lacks enough binder to prevent the colour becoming disturbed by a follow-up process. There are two more satisfactory ways of preparing an oil glaze:

Woodgraining uses a form of colour called a scumble glaze, where the colour pigment has been mixed with a special blend of solvents, binders and paint driers. Transparent scumble glaze does not contain any pigments, and can be used to make up your own glaze, usually using artists' colours. The formulation of a scumble glaze allows it to be spread evenly over a base colour without running, and then be manipulated into a wide variety of effects for at least 20–30 minutes before 'setting'.

Glazes are very slow-drying, but will become less able to manipulate after this period because of solvent evaporation. It takes several days for a glaze to harden completely, and glazes remain vulnerable unless varnished, but this should not take place until after a minimum of a week has elapsed.

Scumble glaze should be easily available from a professional decorating merchant, but it does tend to be expensive. If you use a proprietary brand, follow its instructions regarding thinning, rather than any rule of thumb given here.

You can make your own transparent glaze using the recipe given in Chapter 16. This is an extremely good glaze for relatively small quantities; it does, however, tend to be slower-drying than the proprietary product, and so needs more time for the drying process. (Terebene, which is used in the recipe, is a natural product related to turpentine, derived from the same source; it has the effect of causing the binder – linseed oil – to oxidize with the air faster, and so speeds up the hardening process. It is an important ingredient, but you can live without it if necessary.)

To colour glaze, you need to liquefy artists' oil colour with turps before adding the transparent glaze. You can adjust the depth of colour by adding more colour or more glaze.

Washes These are created by thinning watercolour with water. For our purposes, there is little requirement for them, but it is as well to be aware of their existence. Acrylic watercolours have their own thinning medium, which should be used in preference to plain water.

SURFACE PREPARATION

The same rules generally apply here as with polishing. If there are surface blemishes, they will tend to show through paint just as they show through polish; the difference is that they are easier to deal with.

Holes These may be filled proud of the surface with any proprietary filler such as Polyfilla, and the surplus smoothed away with abrasive paper.

Open grain Very open grain can be a serious drawback when painting, as the pores often show through the paint. Another problem that this open texture presents is that it can spoil a number of effects, particularly those involving glazes, as the pores 'trap' the glaze and make the pores stand out. If the wood is porous, the grain should be filled: it will save a coat or two of paint, as well as improving the surface. Basically, the smoother the surface to be painted, the more effective the final finish will be.

Plywood is particularly bad in this respect, due to the way it is manufactured, which results in a very porous texture (except for the best quality birch or veneer-faced ply).

The most effective way of creating a smooth surface is by using a grain filler in much the same way as you would when French polishing (*see* Chapter 7), leaving out the oiling.

PAINTING THE BASE COLOUR

Only imagination limits the range of decorative effects created by painting wood. There are, however, a number of different techniques that can be learned to form a basic toolkit of methods: a base colour is needed to act as a foundation, and this is normally in an eggshell finish (water- or solvent-based), but because it is a foundation, its application to the substrate should be done with great care. It is essential that the contours of the piece being decorated are not lost, that runs are not allowed and that accumulations in crevices and angles are not allowed to develop. In other words, the furniture must retain its crisp lines, otherwise the painting process will merely create a thick treacly mess, which will only have to be stripped and started again.

Fig 14.2 shows a typical 1930s table with an uninteresting brown finish. Because the surface was basically sound, the varnish was not stripped but given a thorough sanding, to produce a key for painting. Part of the secret is to work logically, dividing the work up into sections. Chapter 8 describes brushwork, and applies equally to painting: two coats of eggshell should be enough to give a smooth surface of solid colour. Fig 14.3 shows the table after two coats of green eggshell and a stencilled decoration (*see* below). This particular colour forms part of a range of over 1000; some of the larger makers of paints operate a colour mixing service by retailers. However, by the very nature of the process, there can be no guarantee that paints mixed at different times will in fact match perfectly, although they have been made to the same specification.

Fig 14.2 A tired 1930s drop-leaf table.

Fig 14.3 The same table rejuvenated with painted decoration.

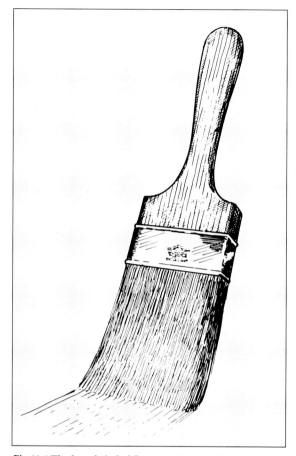

Fig 14.4 The long bristled flogger is designed for dragging.

This problem does not occur with the British Standard colours, of which there are over 100, conforming to BS 4800. The great thing about these is that their exact colour is guaranteed, and so it is possible to match them perfectly. BS 4800 colours extend not just to paints, but to all materials that can be coloured or dyed, and they are used mainly by specifiers – i.e. architects and interior designers – and so fabrics and furniture colours, for example, can be matched.

DRAGGING

A solid base colour may sometimes appear too stark or simply uninteresting, and so will need lifting. Dragging adds a texture akin to graining, by painting a transparent coloured glaze over the dry base colour and then lightly dragging the bristles of a dry brush through the wet glaze in straight lines. The effect can be subtle (using a glaze of similar colour to, but slightly darker than, the base colour), or very obvious (using a glaze whose colour contrasts strongly with the base colour).

Fig 14.5 Green oil glaze dragged over a white eggshell base.

Professionals usually use a special brush, called a flogger (*see* Fig 14.4), for dragging the glaze, but a good quality paintbrush will do the job just as well in most cases – *see* pages 143–4 for descriptions.

The glaze is painted evenly but thinly over the base colour. Use the same principles of dividing up the work as described in Chapter 8. Even though glaze is relatively slow, if it is too thick the lines caused by the dragging brush will fuse together again. After about five minutes' wait, the dragging brush is drawn through the glaze. Fig 14.5 shows a green glaze over a white background. Since glaze is very slow-drying, plenty of time will be needed for it to harden – often as much as several days, during which time it must be kept dust-free.

SPONGING

Fig 14.6(a) shows the broken colour effect of using a natural sponge to manipulate colour on a base coat, with the colour sponged on to the ground; in Fig 14.6(b), a glaze is painted over the ground and the sponge dabbed over the wet glaze to break it up.

The first technique of sponging colour on to the work will produce a crisp, well-defined contrast between ground and top colour. It is ideal for use with water-based colours which dry quickly; for example, acrylic colour can be sponged over an emulsion base.

Sponging colour off the base coat generates a softer, hazier effect. For this you will need an

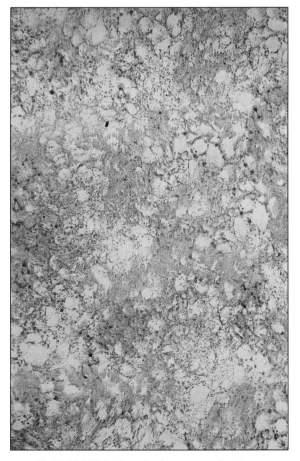

Fig 14.6 (a) Water-based colour sponged on to an emulsion base.

Fig 14.6 (b) The sponge pressed into wet oil glaze over a white eggshell base.

Fig 14.7 Stipple glaze over an eggshell base.

Fig 14.8 Specialist stipple brush used for large areas.

eggshell base coat (either oil- or water-based paint will do for this, as it is the impervious nature of eggshell colour that provides the necessary ground for the glaze). Prepare a glaze as previously described, and paint it fairly thinly over the ground. Allow five minutes or so to pass before taking the sponge (which must be a natural one) and dabbing it into the glaze. You will need to apply some pressure in order to see a reasonable effect. Allow the glaze to dry and harden for a day or so in warm conditions before varnishing.

STIPPLING

An oil glaze is brushed over an eggshell base colour, and after allowing the glaze to settle for about five minutes, the bristle tips of a dry paintbrush are dabbed into it. Fig 14.7 shows the effect as being similar to sponging, but with a more closely spaced pattern.

Special stipple brushes can be used (*see* Fig 14.8); as they are extremely expensive, a good stiff paintbrush will do well for small areas.

RAG-ROLLING

If you pick up colour with a crumpled rag and roll the rag over an emulsion-based colour, you will achieve a similar effect to that seen in Fig 14.9. As with sponging, there is an alternative method, which involves glazing over a base coat of eggshell and rolling a dry rag over it; this creates a softer, subtler effect. Large areas will need to be sectioned off into smaller ones so that the glaze does not 'go off' before you can rag-roll it. Allow the glaze to dry thoroughly before varnishing.

STENCILLING

Stencilling has been an effective means of decoration for many centuries; in its relatively recent revival as an art form, the very best examples of the technique demonstrate a high level of skill in terms of colour and intricacy. However, such skill is not needed to create very pleasant decor-

ative items. Figs 14.2 and 14.3 show how a rather dull and uninteresting piece of furniture can be transformed: the green base colour sets the decorative context, while the stencilled decoration lightens the whole piece.

You can, of course, cut your own stencils using clear acetate sheet and a template (*see* Fig 14.10) but you will need a very sharp craft knife and a pattern that is not so intricate that you will lose definition of the picture. However, there is now a wide range of ready-cut stencils available, so there is little need for making your own, unless you particularly wish to do so.

Stencil paints need to be fast-drying, and so are water-based; special stencil paints are available, but acrylic colours are as good as any. The brushes you use, though, are important; the best results are obtained using proper stencil brushes (*see* Fig 14.11).

Place the stencil over the item, and lightly anchor it with small pieces of masking tape. Pick up the stencil colour with the bristle tips, and dab it on to a clean piece of paper to remove surplus paint. Use a stippling action (*see* Fig 14.12)

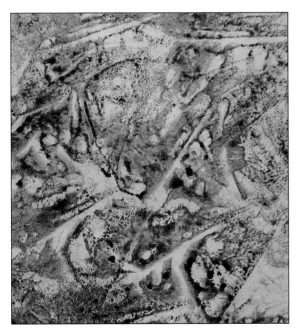

Fig 14.9 (a) Water-based colour rag-rolled on to an emulsion base.

Fig 14.9 (b) The rag rolled in the wet glaze over an eggshell base.

Fig 14.10 Making a stencil using clear acetate sheet with a guiding paper template beneath.

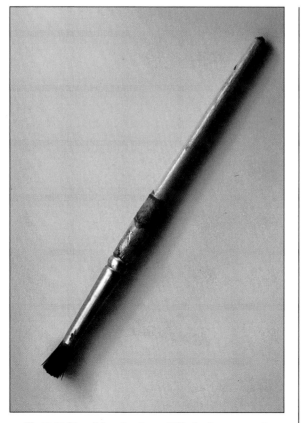

Fig 14.11 Stencil brushes have stiff, short, square-cut bristles designed for the stabbing action.

rather than a brushing one, as it creates a better finish. It is possible to use different colours on different parts of the stencil to create a more interesting and effective decoration (*see* Fig 14.13).

The paint used to stencil must not be thinned, but kept at the consistency as supplied in the container. Thinning will only result in disappointment, as the paint will creep under the edge of the stencil; unthinned acrylic can also be used over eggshell, where a thinned paint will not take. Once the paint has dried it can be varnished.

VARNISHING

All surfaces are vulnerable to natural wear and tear. It is wise to reduce this effect on painted surfaces by applying at least two coats of varnish. (Refer to Chapter 8 on the materials and techniques for varnishing.) A clear varnish is most often used, but it is possible to create interesting effects by using a tinted varnish over stencils or other decorative effects.

Stencilling

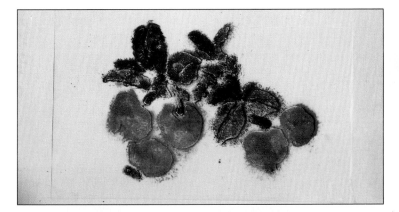

1   Fig 14.12 The stippling action used in stencilling.

2   Fig 14.13 (a) Stencil in place.

3   Fig 14.13 (b) The finished effect.

Limed Oak

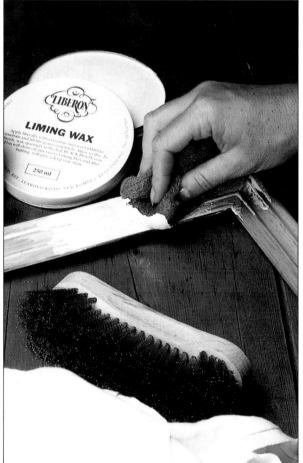

For many centuries lime or chalk has been used for a wide variety of purposes in many trades and crafts. There are the obvious uses in construction, such as cement, mortar, concrete etc., but the less well-known use as a decorative finish is examined here.

The oak panelling in Fig 15.1 illustrates the technique of liming – the deliberate impregnation of lime (or chalk) into the grain. It may seem to be a strange thing to do, but perhaps the following description of the job shown in the photograph will make the point. The house was built in 1840 or thereabouts, in the style of Tudor timber frame with stuccoed brick infill. While the drive up to the house gave an impression of space, this illusion was shattered on walking into the hall: the oak panelling, which was installed in the 1930s, was very dark in colour – a thick coat of deeply coloured varnish obliterated any features in the wood.

The aim of the project was to lighten up the whole area, using only traditional techniques, in such a way that the oak-lined walls formed a backdrop against which furniture, paintings, etc., could be displayed effectively. Liming was the best option.

SURFACE PREPARATION

Oak is the traditional timber for liming because of its open-grained texture, although there is absolutely no reason why any open-grained wood cannot be used, e.g. ash. Large pores are needed to allow the lime to accumulate; this is really important, as the best effect cannot be obtained on close-grained wood.

Some furniture, especially beech-framed chairs, is described by its manufacturers as being limed. In fact, the liming compound has been sprayed on to the work and then rubbed off, leaving deposits in the hollow contours. The effect is rather heavy. Ideally, the lime should only lie in the grain, not on the surface. Badly limed work looks cloudy, and surface preparation is important for providing the right base.

Fig 15.1 Limed oak wall panelling.

Fig 15.2 Using a wire brush to open up the pores.

New or old oak surfaces may be limed. The aim is to make the surface smooth and also to open the pores to help the lime to penetrate. Refer to Chapter 4 for the general method of surface preparation, but note one difference: in order for the liming compound to penetrate the pores of the wood, these need to be opened. This is done by wire brushing along the direction of the grain after sanding. Gently sand afterwards to remove excess roughness (*see* Fig 15.2). Grain opening is particularly important with wood that is being refinished; even after using proprietary stripper there are likely to be deposits of the old finish in the pores.

Always finish off by dusting down with a stiffish brush, to remove sawdust from the pores.

Staining is optional, and depends upon the effect you are trying to achieve. Liming natural oak creates a 'blond' effect, while staining and liming produces a finish with contrast, as shown in Fig 15.3.

Fig 15.3 (a) Blond limed oak.

Fig 15.3 (b) Stained and limed oak.

If the liming compound is put on to the wood at this stage there will be a problem, because some of it will soak into areas other than the pores, making it look very cloudy. This can be overcome by sealing the wood. The easiest way is with white French polish, which should be thinned with 50% meths. Apply it as a thin wash over the whole surface and allow to dry for several hours. This now forms a barrier, but retains the open grain.

LIMING MATERIALS

Here we have a choice. The traditional method involves the use of slaked lime, but this is rather messy and not very pleasant. The alternatives are liming wax or paint.

Liming Wax

While it is feasible to make your own liming wax, there are proprietary brands that will save you the job. As its name implies, the material is a wax-based product that is effectively a wax polish in which is mixed a white pigment, such as zinc oxide.

If you want to make your own, then mix zinc oxide with white spirit to make it fluid before mixing it into wax polish. You may need to thin the wax with turpentine or white spirit until it is very soft.

Apply the paste sparingly and rub well into the grain, finishing off by rubbing across the grain with a clean rag. Ensure that the wax does not accumulate in angles.

Once it has dried, the work can be given a coat of ordinary wax polish.

Paint

Liming wax is ideal for large areas that will not receive any handling, such as wall panelling. However, any item that will need to withstand

Fig 15.4 Wiping off the excess paint.

some wear and tear should not be finished with liming wax, as it will quickly become soiled with handling.

White undercoat is a very effective liming compound for furniture. The important thing to remember is that the wood must be well sealed, because if the paint soaks in, the work will be ruined.

The undercoat must be thinned to a watery consistency with white spirit. The thinned paint is thinly brushed on to the work, but the surplus must be wiped off fairly soon afterwards before it begins to set. Use a rag to clear the surface, leaving the paint in the grain, not on the surface. The rag will need to be changed regularly as it becomes saturated (*see* Fig 15.4).

Finally, the paint is allowed to dry and the work given a very gentle sanding to remove any residue.

FINAL FINISHING

If liming wax has been used, there is little to do in the way of final finishing, other than a dressing with ordinary wax polish. Where paint is used, transparent French polish (without the use of grain filler), clear varnish or synthetic lacquers are suitable.

CHAPTER 16

Recipes
for Finishes

Throughout this book there have been references to a variety of materials that can be bought from the suppliers listed on page 162. However, if you have the time and inclination, many of these materials and products can be made at home, and some of them can *only* be made at home. In fact, should only small quantities be required of, say, oil glaze (gilp), it is probably just as cost-effective to make it yourself.

TACK RAG

A tack rag is used to dust down a surface prior to polishing. The rag has a slightly sticky surface designed to pick up dust without leaving a residue on the surface. It is the woodworker's answer to the damp duster, and ensures that the wood is free of any dust particles that may otherwise become trapped in the film of French polish, varnish or lacquer, and spoil it. A tack rag may be made in the following way:

Piece of stockinette cloth
White spirit or pure turpentine
Raw linseed oil

Soak the cloth in water, and wring it out to dryness. Sprinkle on the white spirit or turpentine, and work it through the whole cloth. Repeat the process with the linseed oil, wringing it out again to ensure there is no surplus liquid. The rag should now be dry to the touch, and should be stored in an airtight jar to prevent it drying out.

During use, after sanding a surface (either the bare wood or after flatting polish), use an ordinary clean duster to remove the worst of the dust before gliding the tack rag over it – use no pressure, but simply wipe it over to lift off any remaining particles.

POLISH REVIVERS

——————— 1 ———————
1 part raw linseed oil
1 part white malt vinegar
1 part methylated spirits

After mixing, the oil will separate out. During use, shake to emulsify. Use the reviver sparingly and apply with a soft cloth, buffing with a clean cloth to finish.

——————— 2 ———————
For polished floors

Equal quantities of paraffin and
white malt vinegar

Shake to emulsify during use, and apply sparingly. Buff with a soft cloth to polish.

——————— 3 ———————
25g beeswax
25g paraffin wax
50g soap
500ml white spirit or pure turpentine
500ml water

This reviver is good for use on fairly heavily soiled surfaces after they have been cleaned with a teaspoon of washing soda in 500ml of warm water.

Dissolve the soap in hot water. Melt the waxes in a double boiler over a low heat; remove from the heat and carefully pour in the white spirit or turps. The wax will immediately set, so return the mixture to a low heat to melt the wax again. Reheat the soap solution and pour it into a container large enough to hold both liquids. Stir the soap continuously as you pour the wax solution into it to form an emulsion. Continue to stir as the mixture cools, to prevent separation. Once cool, pour the creamy liquid into a glass container (plastic will be softened by the turps or white spirit).

The reviver will be ready to use after 24 hours, and sets to a gel. It is used in exactly the same way as other revivers, in that it is applied sparingly with a soft cloth before buffing with a clean cloth. This is a particularly effective reviver, if expensive in terms of time and materials.

WAX POLISH

——— 1 ———

100g white or yellow beeswax
100ml pure turpentine or good quality
white spirit

Melt the wax in a double boiler, and carefully add the turps when all is melted. Continue heating, as the wax will have hardened again. When the mixture has clarified, it can be poured into a permanent container (not plastic, as this will soften) and allowed to set. The polish should be fairly soft (like butter in summer), and it may be necessary to reheat and add a little more turps to soften it, or beeswax to stiffen up a fluid polish.

——— 2 ———

90g beeswax
10g carnauba wax
100ml turpentine

Made up in the same manner as recipe 1, this polish will be slightly stiffer and will yield a harder finish.

Both polishes may be pigmented to create an antiquing wax by stirring in a little raw and burnt umber to the molten waxes. The resulting polish will be a grey/brown colour once it has set. When rubbed into the wood, it imparts a colour cast very like old wood. The wax also collects in crevices and corners, simulating the dirty, dusty effect associated with years of accumulation.

——— 3 ———

Beeswax furniture cream

100g beeswax
100ml turpentine or white spirit
125ml water
0.880 ammonia

The wax is melted as before and dissolved in the turpentine or white spirit. Heat the water, but do not bring it to the boil. When it is hot, quickly pour the wax/turps solution into the water and stir to emulsify it. Add a couple of dashes of the ammonia and continue stirring. The ammonia emulsifies the wax and forms a creamy mixture. Continue stirring until cool, to prevent the mixture separating. This is one of those occasions where a food mixer operating at low speed takes the drudgery out of the work.

When the polish cools it becomes quite creamy in consistency, and should be placed in glass jars. Wax creams are not designed to be used on bare wood, but as a dressing used sparingly over a polished one, such as French polish; the water and ammonia (which acts as an emulsifying agent) actually clean the surface as it polishes. As with all wax polishes, furniture cream should be used sparingly.

OIL POLISH

——— 1 ———

1 part raw linseed oil
8 parts pure turps or good quality white spirit
1 teaspoon terebene for each ½ pint
(0.28l) of mixture
(this is optional, but it does speed up drying)

——— 2 ———

Use food grade oils – corn oil, sunflower, safflower, poppy seed, rapeseed – for salad bowls and any other items used with food.

WOODTURNING WAX STICK

Melt equal quantities of beeswax and carnauba wax in a double boiler. Make a mould out of cooking foil in the shape of a bar, pour in the molten waxes and allow to harden.

FRENCH POLISH

250g shellac flakes
500ml of methylated spirits

The two ingredients are put into a glass or plastic bottle, agitated to mix and then kept in a warm place for at least 24 hours, with occasional shaking; if possible, it is better kept for longer. Strain through a pair of tights and rebottle. It will then be ready to use. This recipe will produce a 4lb (1.81kg) cut polish.

WAX BEAUMONTAGE

Melt equal quantities of beeswax and rosin together in a double boiler (the rosin will take a long time). Melt the rosin first by adding a very small amount of turps. When this has melted, add the beeswax. To colour it, use pure pigments or artists' oil colours. Liquefy the colour with a little turps and pour into the molten wax/rosin; you will need enough colour to make the mixture opaque. After mixing, pour the liquid into foil cake cases and allow to cool. This mixture can be used to cover minor scratches by rubbing the block over the scratch. Allow the deposited wax to harden for a few minutes, and then buff.

TRANSPARENT OIL GLAZE (GILP)

1 part boiled linseed oil
1 part turpentine or white spirit
5ml terebene per 500ml glaze

This gilp is rather fluid, and can only be used if applied thinly, or it will run. It can be thickened up a bit by adding some French chalk: mix in enough to stiffen up the glaze, but not so much as to make it unable to flow off a paint brush. The use of French chalk also has the effect of making the glaze slightly less transparent, and reduces its flow characteristics: as it is brushed on to the work, the glaze does not readily flow into an even film. This property makes it ideal for manipulating into the various effects described in Chapter 14. Gilp without the chalk tends to produce softer results.

Suppliers

Some of the suppliers and manufacturers listed below operate a mail order service, and all provide technical information about their products. The list is by no means exhaustive, but it is a starting point.

Binks-Bullows Ltd
Pelsall Road, Brownhills, Walsall WS8 7HW
Major manufacturer of spray technology.

Clarke Group
Lower Clapton Road, London E5 0QR
Spray equipment manufacturers and suppliers.

Craft Supplies Ltd
The Mill, Millers Dale, Buxton SK17 8SN
Suppliers of woodturning tools and equipment; also stock a wide range of finishing materials. (Mail order.)

Cuprinol Ltd
Adderwell, Frome, Somerset BA11 1NL
Preservatives and woodfinishing products.

DeVilbiss Ransburg
Ringwood Road, Bournemouth, Dorset BH1 9LH
Major manufacturer of spray technology.

Fiddes & Son Ltd
Trade Street, Cardiff
Full range of materials for the woodfinisher.

Hamilton Acorn Ltd
Halford Road, Attleborough, Norfolk NR17 2HZ
Manufacturer of brushes for finishing.

John Myland Ltd
80 Norwood High Street, London SE27 9BP
A comprehensive range of finishing materials and tools for traditional and modern finishing. (Mail order.)

Liberon Waxes
Mountfield Industrial Estate, Learoyd Road, New Romney, Kent TN28 8XU
Full range of traditional finishing materials.

Rentokil Advice Centre
Freepost, East Grinstead, West Sussex RH19 2BR
Provides information on dealing with wood infestation.

Restoration Materials
Proctor Street, Bury, Lancs.
Full range of finishing and restoration materials. (Mail order.)

Rustin's Ltd
Waterloo Road, Cricklewood, London NW2 7TX
Manufacture a wide range of finishing products.

Sonneborn & Riek Ltd
91-95 Peregrine Road, Hainault, Ilford, Essex
Manufacturer and supplier of modern finishing materials.

Metric Conversion Table

INCHES TO MILLIMETRES AND CENTIMETRES

MM = Millimetres   CM = Centimetres

INCHES	MM	CM	INCHES	CM	INCHES	CM
⅛	3	0.3	9	22.9	30	76.2
¼	6	0.6	10	25.4	31	78.7
⅜	10	1.0	11	27.9	32	81.3
½	13	1.3	12	30.5	33	83.8
⅝	16	1.6	13	33.0	34	86.4
¾	19	1.9	14	35.6	35	88.9
⅞	22	2.2	15	38.1	36	91.4
1	25	2.5	16	40.6	37	94.0
1¼	32	3.2	17	43.2	38	96.5
1½	38	3.8	18	45.7	39	99.1
1¾	44	4.4	19	48.3	40	101.6
2	51	5.1	20	50.8	41	104.1
2½	64	6.4	21	53.3	42	106.7
3	76	7.6	22	55.9	43	109.2
3½	89	8.9	23	58.4	44	111.8
4	102	10.2	24	61.0	45	114.3
4½	114	11.4	25	63.5	46	116.8
5	127	12.7	26	66.0	47	119.4
6	152	15.2	27	68.6	48	121.9
7	178	17.8	28	71.1	49	124.5
8	203	20.3	29	73.7	50	127.0

About the Author

Ian Hosker began learning his craft at the age of 14 from his grandfather, whose range of skills seemed at the time to be awesome. What at first was natural adolescent curiosity became something of a passion as interest and skill grew – a phenomenon that many workers in wood will be familiar with. The channel for this passion was a business in furniture restoration and cabinetmaking, that ran alongside a career in mainstream education. His clients include interior designers (some with very distinguished clients themselves, offering the opportunity to work on some very fine pieces) as well as private commissions.

Now, living in Devon with his wife, Barbara, and children, Samantha and David, he writes, teaches and demonstrates extensively on the subject of furniture – its history, construction and repair – while at the same time fulfilling his fantasy as a salty sea-dog. Furniture, however, remains his all-abiding passion.

Index

Other Titles Available
From GMC Publications Ltd

GMC Publications regularly produces new books on a wide range of woodworking and craft subjects, and an increasing number of specialist magazines, all available on subscription:

MAGAZINES

Furniture   Woodturning   Woodcarving   Businessmatters

All these books and magazines are available through bookshops and newsagents, or may be ordered by post from the publishers at 166 High Street, Lewes, East Sussex BN7 1XU, telephone (0273) 477374. Credit card orders are accepted. Please write or phone for the latest information.